THE RICHARD ELLMANN LECTURES
IN MODERN LITERATURE

Confessions of a Young Novelist

Umberto Eco

Harvard University Press

CAMBRIDGE, MASSACHUSETTS

LONDON, ENGLAND

2011

Copyright © 2011 by the President and Fellows of Harvard College
Printed in the United States of America

Library of Congress Cataloging-in-Publication Data

Eco, Umberto.
    Confessions of a young novelist / Umberto Eco.
        p. cm.—(The Richard Ellmann lectures in modern literature)
    Includes bibliographical references and index.
    ISBN 978-0-674-05869-9 (alk. paper)
    1. Eco, Umberto—Authorship.   I. Title.
    PQ4865.C6Z46 2011
    853′.914—dc22
    [B]   2010033172

Book design by Dean Bornstein

Contents

Confessions of a Young Novelist

Writing from Left to Right

These lectures are entitled *Confessions of a Young Novelist*—and one might well ask why, since I am marching toward my seventy-seventh year. But it so happens that I published my first novel, *The Name of the Rose,* in 1980, which means that I started my career as a novelist a mere twenty-eight years ago. Thus, I consider myself a very young and certainly promising novelist, who has so far published only five novels and will publish many more in the next fifty years. This work in progress is still unfinished (otherwise it wouldn't be in progress), but I hope I have amassed enough experience to say a few words about the way I write. In line with the spirit of the Richard Ellmann Lectures, I shall focus on my fiction rather than on my essays, though I view myself as an academic by profession, and as a novelist only an amateur.

I began to write novels in my childhood. The first thing I would come up with was the title, usually inspired by the adventure books of those days, which were much like *Pirates of the Caribbean.* I would im-

CONFESSIONS OF A YOUNG NOVELIST

mediately draw all of the illustrations, then start the first chapter. But since I always wrote in block capitals, in imitation of printed books, I would become exhausted after just a few pages and would give up. Each of my works was thus an unfinished masterpiece, like Schubert's *Unfinished Symphony*.

At sixteen, I of course began to write poems, like every other teenager. I do not remember whether it was the need for poetry that caused the flowering of my first (platonic and unconfessed) love, or vice versa. The mixture was a disaster. But as I once wrote—though in the form of a paradox uttered by one of my fictional characters—there are two kinds of poets: good ones, who burn their poems at the age of eighteen, and bad ones, who keep writing poetry for as long as they live.[1]

What Is Creative Writing?

When I reached my early fifties, I did not, as many scholars do, feel frustrated by the fact that my writing wasn't the "creative" sort.[2]

I have never understood why Homer is viewed as a creative writer and Plato isn't. Why is a bad poet a creative writer, while a good scientific essayist is not?

In French, you can make a distinction between an

2

écrivain—someone who produces "creative" texts, such as a novelist or a poet—and an *écrivant:* somebody who records facts, such as a bank clerk, or a cop preparing a criminal-case report. But what kind of writer is a philosopher? We might say that a philosopher is a professional writer whose texts can be summarized or translated into other words without losing all of their meaning, whereas the texts of creative writers cannot be fully translated or paraphrased. But although it is certainly difficult to translate poetry and novels, ninety percent of the world's readers have read *War and Peace* or *Don Quixote* in translation; and I think that a translated Tolstoy is more faithful to the original than any English translation of Heidegger or Lacan. Is Lacan more "creative" than Cervantes?

The difference cannot even be expressed in terms of the social function of a given text. Galileo's texts are certainly of major philosophical and scientific importance, but in Italian high schools they are studied as examples of fine creative writing—as masterpieces of style.

Suppose you are a librarian, and you decide to put the so-called creative texts in Room A and the so-called scientific texts in Room B. Would you group Einstein's essays with Edison's letters to his sponsors, and "Oh, Susanna!" with *Hamlet?*

Somebody has suggested that "noncreative" writers such as Linnaeus and Darwin wanted to convey true information about whales or apes, whereas when Melville wrote about a white whale and Burroughs told of Tarzan of the Apes, they only *pretended* to state the truth but in fact were inventing nonexistent whales and apes and had no interest in the real ones. Can we say without a doubt that Melville, in telling the story of a nonexistent whale, had no intention of saying anything true about life and death, or about human pride and obstinacy?

It is problematic to define as "creative" a writer who simply tells us things which are contrary to fact. Ptolemy said something untrue about the movement of the Earth. Should we then claim that he was more creative than Kepler?

The difference lies, rather, in the contrasting ways in which writers can respond to interpretations of their texts. If I said to a philosopher, to a scientist, to an art critic, "You have written thus-and-such," the author can always retort, "You misunderstood my text. I said exactly the opposite." But if a critic offered a Marxist interpretation of *In Search of Lost Time*—say, that at the peak of the crisis of the decadent bourgeoisie, total devotion to the realm of memory necessarily isolated the artist from society

—Proust might be dissatisfied with this interpretation, but would have difficulty refuting it.

As we shall see in a subsequent lecture, creative writers—as reasonable readers of their own work—certainly have the right to challenge a farfetched interpretation. But in general they must respect their readers, since they've thrown their text out into the world like a message in a bottle, so to speak.

After I publish a text on semiotics, I devote my time either to recognizing that I was wrong or to demonstrating that those who did not understand it in the way I meant were misreading it. In contrast, after I publish a novel, I feel in principle a moral duty not to challenge people's interpretations of it (and not to encourage any).

This happens—and here we can identify the real difference between creative and scientific writing—because, in a theoretical essay, one usually wants to demonstrate a particular thesis or to give an answer to a specific problem. Whereas in a poem or a novel, one wants to represent life with all its inconsistency. One wants to stage a series of contradictions, making them evident and poignant. Creative writers ask their readers to try a solution; they do not offer a definite formula (except for kitschy and sentimental writers, who are aiming to offer cheap consolation). That is why, in the days when I was giving talks about my newly published first novel, I said that sometimes a novelist can say things that a philosopher cannot.

Thus, until 1978 I felt totally fulfilled being a philosopher and a semiotician. Once I even wrote—with a touch of Platonic arrogance—that I considered poets, and artists in general, as prisoners of their own lies, imitators of imitations; while as a philosopher I had access to the true Platonic World of Ideas.

One could say that, creativity aside, many scholars have felt the impulse to tell stories and have regretted being unable to do so—and that this is why the desk drawers of many university professors are full of bad unpublished novels. But over the years I satisfied my secret passion for narrative in two different ways: first, by often engaging in oral narrativity, telling stories to my children (so that I was at a loss when they grew up and shifted from fairy tales to rock music); second, by making a narrative out of every critical essay.

When I presented my doctoral dissertation on the aesthetics of Thomas Aquinas—a very controversial subject, since at that time scholars believed there were no aesthetic reflections in his immense body of work—one of my examiners charged me with a sort of "narrative fallacy." He said that a mature scholar, when setting out to do some research, inevitably proceeds by trial and error, making and rejecting different hypotheses; but at the end of the inquiry, all those attempts should have been digested and the scholar should present only the conclusions. In contrast, he said, I told the story of my research as if it were a detective novel. The objection was made in a friendly manner, and suggested to me the fundamental idea that *all research findings must be "narrated" this way.* Every scientific book must be a sort of whodunnit—the report of a quest for some Holy Grail. And I think I have done this in all my subsequent academic works.

Once Upon a Time

In early 1978, a friend of mine who worked for a small publisher told me that she was asking non-novelists (philosophers, sociologists, politicians, and so on) to each write a short detective story. For the reasons I have just mentioned, I replied that I was not interested in creative writing, and that I was sure I was absolutely incapable of writing good dialogue. I concluded (I do not know why) by saying provocatively that if I had to write a crime novel, it would be at least five hundred pages long and would be set in a medieval monastery. My friend said she was not fishing for an ungainly potboiler, and our meeting ended there.

As soon as I returned home, I hunted through my desk drawers and retrieved a scribbling from the previous year—a piece of paper on which I had written down some names of monks. It meant that in the most secret part of my soul the idea for a novel had already been growing, but I was unaware of it. At that point, I had realized it would be nice to poison a monk while he was reading a mysterious book, and that was all. Now I started to write *The Name of the Rose.*

After the book was published, people often asked me why I had decided to write a novel, and the reasons I gave (which varied according to my mood) were probably all true—meaning that they were all false. Eventually I realized the only correct answer was that at a certain moment of my life I felt the urge to do it—and I think this is a sufficient and reasonable explanation.

How To Write

When interviewers ask me, "How did you write your novels?" I usually cut short this line of questioning and reply, "From left to right." I realize that this is not a satisfactory answer, and that it can produce some astonishment in Arab countries and in Israel. Now I have time for a more detailed response.

In the course of writing my first novel, I learned a few things. First, "inspiration" is a bad word that tricky authors use in order to seem artistically respectable. As the old adage goes, genius is ten percent inspiration and ninety percent perspiration. It is said that the French poet Lamartine often described the circumstances in which he had written one of his best poems: he claimed it had come to him fully formed in a sudden illumination, one night when he was wandering through the woods. After his death, somebody found in his study an impressive number of versions of that poem, which he had written and rewritten over the course of years.

The first critics who reviewed *The Name of the Rose* said it had been written under the influence of a luminous inspiration, but that, because of its conceptual and linguistic difficulties, it was only for the happy few. When the book met with remarkable success, selling millions of copies, the same critics wrote that in order to concoct such a popular and entertaining bestseller, I had no doubt mechanically followed a secret recipe. Later they said the key to the book's success was a computer program—forgetting that the first personal computers with viable writing software appeared only at the beginning of the 1980s, when my novel was already in print. In 1978–1979, all you could find, even in the United States, were cheap little computers made by Tandy, and no one would ever have used them to write anything more than a letter.

Some time afterward, a little upset by those computer allegations, I formulated the real recipe for writing a computer-made bestseller:

First of all you need a computer, obviously, which is an intelligent machine that thinks for you. This would be a definite advantage for many people. All you need is a program of a few lines; even a child could do it. Then one feeds into the computer the content of a hundred or so novels, scientific works, the Bible, the Koran, and a bunch of telephone directories (very useful for characters' names). Say, something like 120,000 pages. After this, using another program, you randomize; in other words, you mix all those texts together, making some adjustments—for instance, eliminating all the *e*'s—in order to have not only a novel but a Perec-like lipogram. At this point, you click on "Print," and, since you have eliminated all the *e*'s, what comes out is something less than 120,000 pages. After you have read them carefully several times, underlining the most significant passages, you take them to an incinerator. Then you simply sit under a tree, with a piece of charcoal and good-quality drawing paper in hand, and, allowing your mind to wander, you write down two lines—for instance: "The moon is high in the sky/The wood rustles." Maybe what emerges initially is not a novel, but rather a Japanese haiku. Nevertheless, the important thing is to get started.[3]

Speaking of slow inspiration, *The Name of the Rose* took me only two years to write, for the simple reason that I did not need to do any research on the Middle Ages. As I said, my doctoral dissertation was on medieval aesthetics, and I devoted further study to the Middle Ages. Over the years, I visited a lot of Romanesque abbeys, Gothic cathedrals, and so on. When I decided to write the novel, it was as if I had opened a big closet where I had been piling up my medieval files for decades. All that material was there at my feet, and I had only to select what I needed. For the subsequent novels, the situation was different (though if I selected a given subject, it was because I already had some familiarity with it). That is why my later novels took a lot of time—eight years for *Foucault's Pendulum,* six for *The Island of the Day Before* and for *Baudolino.* I spent only four on *The Mysterious Flame of Queen Loana,* because it deals with my readings as a child in the 1930s and 1940s, and I was able to use a lot of old material I had at home, such as comic strips, recordings, magazines, and newspapers—in short, my entire collection of mementos, nostalgia, and trivia.

Building a World

What do I do during the years of literary pregnancy? I collect documents; I visit places and draw maps; I note the layouts of buildings, or perhaps a ship, as in the case of the *Island of the Day Before;* and I sketch the faces of characters. For *The Name of the Rose*, I made portraits of all the monks I was writing about. I spend those preparatory years in a sort of enchanted castle—or, if you prefer, in a state of autistic withdrawal. Nobody knows what I am doing, not even the members of my family. I give the impression of doing a lot of different things, but I am always focused on capturing ideas, images, words for my story. If, while writing on the Middle Ages, I see a car passing on the street and am perhaps impressed by its color, I record the experience in my notebook, or simply in my mind, and that color will later play a role in the description of, say, a miniature.

When planning *Foucault's Pendulum,* I spent evening after evening, right until closing time, walking through the corridors of the Conservatoire des Arts et Métiers, where some of the main events of the story take place. In order to describe Casaubon's nighttime walk through Paris, from the Conservatoire to the Place des Vosges and then to the Eiffel Tower, I spent a number of nights roaming the city between two and three in the morning, dictating into a pocket tape recorder everything I could see, so as not to get the street names and intersections wrong.

When preparing to write *The Island of the Day Before*, I naturally went to the South Seas, to the precise geographic location where the book is set, to see the colors of the water and sky at different hours of the day, and the tints of the fishes and corals. But I also spent two or three years studying drawings and models of ships of the period, to find out how big a cabin or cubbyhole was, and how a person could move from one to the other.

After the publication of *The Name of the Rose*, the first movie director who proposed making a film out of it was Marco Ferreri. He told me, "Your book seems conceived expressly for a movie script, since the dialogues are just the right length." At first, I did not understand why. Then I remembered that before I'd begun writing, I had drawn hundreds of labyrinths and plans of abbeys, so that I knew how long it would take two characters to go from one place to another, conversing as they went. Thus, the layout of my fictional world dictated the length of the dialogues.

In this way, I learned that a novel is not just a linguistic phenomenon. In poetry, words are difficult to translate because what counts there is their sound, as well as their deliberately multiple meanings, and it is the choice of words that determines the content. In narrative, we have the opposite situation: it is the *universe* the author has built, and the events that occur in it, that dictate rhythm, style, and even word choice. Narrative is governed by the Latin rule, "Rem tene, verba sequentur"—"Stick with the subject and the words will follow"—whereas in poetry we should change this to, "Stick with the words and the subject will follow."

Narrative is, first and foremost, a cosmological affair. To narrate something, you start as a sort of demiurge who creates a world—a world that must be as precise as possible, so that you can move around in it with total confidence.

I follow this rule so closely that, for instance, when in *Foucault's Pendulum* I say that the publishing houses of Manuzio and Garamond are in two adjoining buildings, between which a passageway has been built, I spent a long time drawing several plans and working out what that passageway looked like, and whether there had to be some steps to compensate for the difference in height between the buildings. In the novel, I briefly mention the steps, and the reader takes them in stride without, I think, paying much attention to them. But for me they were crucial, and if I had not designed them I would have been unable to go on with my story.

People say that Luchino Visconti did something similar in his movies. When the script called for two characters to talk about a box of jewels, he insisted that the box, even though it was never opened, actually contain authentic jewels. Otherwise, the actors would have performed with less conviction.

The readers of *Foucault's Pendulum* are not supposed to know the precise layout of the publishing-house offices. Although the structure of a novel's world—the setting for the events and characters of the story—is fundamental for the writer, it often must remain imprecise for the reader. In *The Name of the Rose,* however, there is a plan of the abbey at the beginning of the book. This is a puckish reference to the many old-fashioned detective novels that include a plan of the crime scene (say, a vicarage or manor house), and is a sort of ironic mark of realism, a bit of "evidence" proving that the abbey really existed. But I also wanted my readers to visualize clearly how my characters moved through the monastery.

After the publication of *The Island of the Day*

Before, my German publisher asked me whether it wouldn't be helpful if the novel included a diagram showing the layout of the ship. I did have such a diagram, and I'd spent a lot of time designing it, just as I had with the plan of the abbey for *The Name of the Rose.* But in the case of *The Island,* I wanted the reader to be confused—and also the hero, who is unable to find his way around that labyrinth of a ship, often exploring it after generous alcoholic libations. Thus, I needed to bamboozle my reader while keeping my own ideas very clear—always referring, as I wrote, to spaces that were calculated down to the last millimeter.

Seminal Ideas

Another frequently asked question is: "What rough idea or detailed plan do you have in your mind when you start writing?" Only after my third novel did I fully realize that each of my novels grew out of a seminal idea that was little more than an image. In *Reflections on "The Name of the Rose,"* I said that I'd begun writing that novel because "I wanted to poison a monk." Actually, I had no desire to poison a monk—I mean, I've never wanted to poison anyone, whether monk or secular person. I was simply struck by the image of a monk poisoned while reading a book. Perhaps I was remembering an experience I'd had at the age of sixteen: visiting a Benedictine monastery (Santa Scolastica at Subiaco), I'd walked through the medieval cloisters and entered a dark library, where, open on a lectern, I'd found the *Acta Sanctorum*. Browsing through that enormous volume in profound silence, while a few beams of light filtered through the stained-glass windows, I must have felt something like a thrill. More than forty years later, that thrill emerged from my unconscious.

This was the seminal image. The rest came bit by bit, in my striving to make sense of that image. And it came on its own, gradually, as I rummaged through twenty-five years' worth of old filing cards on the Middle Ages, originally intended for a completely different purpose.

With *Foucault's Pendulum*, things were more complicated. After writing *The Name of the Rose*, I had the feeling that I'd put into my first (and maybe last) novel everything that, even indirectly, I could say about myself. Was there anything else truly my own that I could write about? Two images came to my mind.

The first was that of Léon Foucault's pendulum, which I had seen thirty years before in Paris and which had made a huge impression on me—another thrill that had long been buried in the depths of my soul. The second image was that of myself playing the trumpet at a funeral for members of the Italian Resistance. A true story which I had never stopped telling, because I found it beautiful—and also because, when I later read Joyce, I realized that I had experienced what he calls (in *Stephen Hero*) an epiphany.

Thus, I decided to tell a story starting with the pendulum and ending with a little trumpeter in a cemetery on a sunny morning. But how to get from the pendulum to the trumpet? To answer this question took me eight years, and the answer was the novel.

With *The Island of the Day Before,* I started from a question posed by a French journalist: "Why do you describe spaces so well?" I had never paid attention to my description of spaces, but by reflecting on that question I realized what I have already said—namely, that if you design every detail of a world, you know how to describe it in terms of space, since you have it before your eyes. There was a classical literary genre called *ekphrasis* which consisted in describing a given image (a painting or a statue) so carefully that even those who had never laid eyes on it could see it as if it were in front of them. As Joseph Addison wrote in *The Pleasures of the Imagination* (1712), "Words, when well chosen, have so great a Force in them, that a Description often gives us more lively Ideas than the Sight of Things themselves." It is said that when the *Laocoön* was discovered in Rome in 1506, people recognized it as that famous Greek statue because of the verbal description provided by Pliny the Elder in his *Naturalis Historia.*

So why not tell a story in which space played an important role? Moreover (I told myself), in my first two novels I'd spoken too much about monasteries and museums—that is, about closed cultural spaces. I should try to write about open, natural spaces. And how could I fill a novel with enormous spaces —nature and nothing else? By placing my hero on a desert island.

At the same time, I was intrigued by one of those world clocks which give the local time for every spot on the globe and display a sign indicating the International Date Line, on the one hundred eightieth meridian. Everybody knows that this line exists, because everybody has read Jules Verne's *Around the World in Eighty Days,* but we do not often think of it.

Well, my protagonist had to be west of that line and see an island to the east, where it was one day earlier. He could not be shipwrecked on the island itself but had to be marooned within view of it, and he had to be unable to swim, so that he would be forced to gaze at the island that was distant from him in space and time.

My clock showed that one such fateful point was in the Aleutian Islands, but I did not know how I could arrange to have a character get stuck there. Could I shipwreck my hero on an oil rig? I said above that when I am writing about a specific place, I need to be there, and the idea of going to a chilly region like the Aleutians did not appeal to me at all.

Yet as I pondered the problem and leafed through my atlas, I discovered that the Date Line also passed through the Fijian archipelago. The South Pacific islands had rich associations with Robert Louis Stevenson. Many of these lands had become known to Europeans in the seventeenth century; I knew Baroque culture pretty well—those were the days of the Three Musketeers and Cardinal Richelieu. I had only to start, and then the novel could walk on its own two feet.

Once an author has designed a specific narrative world, the words will follow, and they will be those that the particular world requires. For this reason, the style I used in *The Name of the Rose* was that of a medieval chronicler: precise, naive, flat when necessary (a humble fourteenth-century monk does not write like Joyce, or remember things like Proust). Moreover, since I was supposedly transcribing from a nineteenth-century translation of a medieval text, the stylistic model was only indirectly the Latin of the medieval chroniclers of the time; the more immediate model was the style of their modern translators.

In *Foucault's Pendulum,* a plurality of languages had to come into play: Agliè's educated and archaizing language, Ardenti's pseudo-D'Annunzian fascist rhetoric, the disenchanted and ironically literary language of Belbo's secret files (really postmodern in its frenetic use of literary quotations), Garamond's kitschy style, and the bawdy dialogues of the three editors during their irresponsible fantasies, mixing learned references with sophomoric puns. Those "leaps of register" did not depend on a simple stylistic choice, but were determined by the nature of the world in which the events took place and by the psychology of the characters.

In *The Island of the Day Before,* the cultural period was the determining factor. It influenced not just the style but the very structure of the ongoing dialogue between narrator and character, while the reader is continually appealed to as a witness and accomplice in that dispute. This sort of metanarrative choice resulted from the fact that my characters were supposed to speak in a Baroque style, though I myself could not. So I had to have a narrator of many moods and functions: at times he gets irritated by the verbal excesses of his characters; at other times, he is their victim; and at still other times, he tempers those excesses by apologizing to the reader.

So far, I have said that (1) my starting point is a seminal idea or image, and (2) the construction of the narrative world determines the novel's style. My fourth venture into fiction, *Baudolino*, contradicts these two principles. Regarding the seminal idea: for at least two years, I had a number of them—and if there are too many seminal ideas, this is a sign that they are not seminal. At a certain point, I decided that my protagonist would be a little boy born in Alessandria, my native city, founded in the twelfth century and besieged by Frederick Barbarossa. Furthermore, I wanted my Baudolino to be the son of the legendary Gagliaudo, who, when Frederick Barbarossa was on the verge of conquering the city, foiled him through a malicious trick, a lie, a fraud —and if you want to know what it was, read the book.

Baudolino was a good opportunity to return to my beloved Middle Ages, to my personal roots, to my fascination with fakes. But this was not enough. I did not know how to start, what kind of style to use, or who my real hero was.

I reflected on the fact that in those days, in my native region, people no longer spoke Latin but used new dialects that in some ways resembled today's Italian language, which was then in its infancy. But we have no records of the dialect spoken in those years in northeastern Italy. Thus, I felt free to invent a popular idiom, a hypothetical twelfth-century Po Valley pidgin; and I think I worked it out pretty well, because a friend of mine who teaches a course in the history of the Italian language told me that— although nobody can confirm or challenge my invention—Baudolino's language was not improbable.

This language, which posed no small problems for my courageous translators, suggested to me the psychology of my protagonist, Baudolino, and made my fourth novel a picaresque counterpoint to *The Name of the Rose.* The latter was a story of intellectuals speaking in high style, whereas *Baudolino* dealt with peasants, warriors, and impudent Goliards. Thus, the style I adopted determined the story I would tell.

I must acknowledge, however, that *Baudolino* likewise depends on a first, poignant image. I had long been fascinated by Constantinople, which I had never seen. In order to have a reason to visit it, I needed to tell a story about this city and the Byzantine civilization. So I went to Constantinople. I explored its surface and the layers beneath, and I found the starting image for my story: the city being set on fire by the Crusaders in 1204.

Take Constantinople in flames, a young liar, a German emperor, and some Asian monsters, and you have the novel. I admit that this does not sound like a convincing recipe, but for me it worked.

I must add that by reading widely on Byzantine culture, I discovered Niketas Choniates, a Greek historian of that period, and I decided to tell the whole story as a report by Baudolino—a supposed liar—to Niketas. I also had my metanarrative structure: a story in which not only Niketas but even the narrator and the reader are never sure of what Baudolino is recounting.

Constraints

I said above that once I have found the seminal image, the story can move forward on its own. This is true only to a certain extent. In order to enable the story to proceed, the writer must impose some constraints.

Constraints are fundamental to every artistic endeavor. A painter who decides to use oils rather than tempera, a canvas rather than a wall; a composer who opts for a given key; a poet who chooses to use rhyming couplets, or hendecasyllables rather than alexandrines—all establish a system of constraints. So do avant-garde artists, who seem to avoid constraints; they simply construct others, which go unnoticed.

To choose the seven trumpets of the Apocalypse as a scheme for the succession of events, as I did in *The Name of the Rose,* is a constraint. Another would be to set a story at a precise time, because in a certain historical period you can make some things happen but not others. It was a constraint to decide that, in line with the occult obsessions of some of my characters, *Foucault's Pendulum* needed to have precisely one hundred twenty chapters, and that the story had to be divided into ten parts, like the Sephiroth of the Kabbalah.

Another constraint on *Foucault's Pendulum* was that the characters had to have lived through the student protests of 1968. But Belbo then writes his files on his computer—which also plays a formal role in the story, by partly inspiring its aleatory and combinatory nature—so the final events could take place only at the beginning of the 1980s and not before, since the first personal computers with word-processing programs went on sale in Italy in 1982–1983. But in order to allow time to elapse from 1968 to 1983, I was forced to send my hero, Casaubon, somewhere else. Where? My memories of some magic rituals which I had witnessed brought me back to Brazil, where I set Casaubon for more than ten years. Many found this an overly long digression, but for me (and for some benevolent readers) it was essential, because what happens in Brazil is a sort of hallucinated premonition of what will happen to my characters in the rest of the book.

If IBM or Apple had started selling good word-processors six or seven years earlier, my novel would have been different. There would have been no Brazil—and from my point of view, that would have been a great loss.

The Island of the Day Before was based on a series of temporal constraints. For instance, I wanted my hero, Roberto, to be in Paris on the day of Richelieu's death (December 4, 1642). Was it necessary for Roberto to be present at Richelieu's death? Not at all; my story would have been the same even if Roberto did not see Richelieu in his deathbed agony. Moreover, when I introduced that constraint, I had no thoughts as to its possible function. I just wanted to represent Richelieu on the verge of dying. It was simply sadism.

But that constraint obliged me to solve a puzzle. Roberto had to arrive on his island in August of the following year because that was the month when I had visited those islands, and I was able to describe sunrises in nocturnal skies only at that season. It was not impossible that a sailing ship could go from Europe to Melanesia in six or seven months, but at this point I had to face a tremendous difficulty: after August, somebody had to find Roberto's diary on what remained of the ship that hosted him. But the Dutch explorer Abel Tasman probably reached the Fiji Islands before June—that is, before Roberto's arrival. This explains the hints I inserted in the final chapter, to persuade the reader that perhaps Tasman had passed twice though that archipelago without registering the second visit in his logbook (so that both author and reader are induced to imagine silences, conspiracies, ambiguities), or that Captain Bligh docked at the island when escaping from the Bounty mutiny (a more fascinating hypothesis, and a fine and ironic way to merge two textual universes).

My novel relies on many other constraints, but I

cannot reveal all of them. In order to write a successful novel, one needs to keep certain recipes secret.

As for *Baudolino*, I said that I wanted to begin the story with Constantinople in flames, in 1204. Since I intended to have Baudolino forge a letter by Prester John and take part in the founding of Alessandria, I was obliged to make his birthdate around 1142, so that in 1204 he is already sixty-two. In this sense, the story had to start from its endpoint, with Baudolino telling about his past adventures through a series of flashbacks. No problem.

But Baudolino finds himself in Constantinople on his way back from the kingdom of Prester John. Now, the false letter of the Priest was—historically speaking—forged or disseminated around 1160, and in my novel Baudolino writes it to convince Frederick Barbarossa to advance toward that mysterious kingdom. So, even if Baudolino were to spend fifteen years or so traveling to the kingdom, staying there, and escaping from thousands of adventures, he could not start his pilgrimage before 1198 (also, it has been historically demonstrated that Barbarossa moved toward the East only in that year). Then what the hell could I make Baudolino do between 1160 and 1190? Why couldn't he start his exploration immediately after disseminating the letter? It was a bit like the business of the computer in *Foucault's Pendulum.*

Thus, I was obliged to keep him occupied, and I made him continually delay his departure. I had to invent a series of accidents in order to arrive finally at the end of the century. Yet it is only by doing so that the novel creates—not only in Baudolino but also in its readers—the Twinge of Desire. Baudolino yearns for the kingdom, but must constantly postpone his search. So Prester John's kingdom grows as an object of Baudolino's longing, and, I hope, as an object of readerly desire as well. Once more, the advantages of constraints.

Double Coding

I do not belong to that gang of bad writers who say that they write only for themselves. The only things that writers write for themselves are shopping lists, which help them to remember what to buy, and then can be thrown away. All the rest, including laundry lists, are messages addressed to somebody else. They are not monologues; they are dialogues.

Now, some critics have found that my novels contain a typical postmodern feature—namely, double coding.[4]

I was aware from the beginning—and I said this

in *Reflections on "The Name of the Rose"*—that, whatever postmodernism might be, I use at least two typical postmodern techniques. One is intertextual irony: direct quotations from other famous texts, or more or less transparent references to them. The second is metanarrative: reflections that the text makes on its own nature, when the author speaks directly to the reader.

"Double coding" is the concurrent use of intertextual irony and an implicit metanarrative appeal. The term was coined by the architect Charles Jencks, for whom postmodern architecture "speaks on at least two levels at once: to other architects and a concerned minority who care about specifically architectural meanings, and to the public at large, or the local inhabitants, who care about other issues concerned with comfort, traditional building and a way of life."[5] He defines it further: "The postmodern building or work of art addresses simultaneously a minority, elite public using 'high' codes, and a mass public using popular codes."[6]

Let me cite an example of double coding from my own novels. *The Name of the Rose* begins by telling how the author came across an ancient medieval text. It is a blatant case of intertextual irony, since the topos (that is, the literary commonplace) of the rediscovered manuscript has a venerable pedigree. The

irony is double, and is also a metanarrative sugges-
tion, since the text claims that the manuscript was
available through a nineteenth-century translation
of the original manuscript—a remark that justifies
some elements of the neo-Gothic novel which are
present in the story. Naive or popular readers cannot
enjoy the narrative that follows unless they are aware
of this game of Chinese boxes, this regression of
sources, which gives the story an aura of ambiguity.

But if you remember, the heading on the page
which talks about the medieval source is "Naturally,
a Manuscript." The word "Naturally" should have a
particular effect on sophisticated readers, who now
are bound to realize that they are dealing with a
literary topos, and that the author is revealing his
"anxiety of influence," since (at least for Italian readers) the intended reference is to the greatest Italian
novelist of the nineteenth century, Alessandro Man-
zoni, who begins his book *The Betrothed* by claiming a seventeenth-century manuscript as his source.
How many readers could grasp the ironic resonances
of that "Naturally"? Not many, since a lot of them
wrote to me asking if that manuscript really existed.
But if they have not grasped the allusion, will they
still be able to appreciate the rest of the story and get
most of its flavor? I think they will. They have merely
lost an additional wink.

I admit that by employing this double-coding technique, the author establishes a sort of silent complicity with the sophisticated reader, and that some popular readers, when they do not get the cultivated allusion, may feel that something is escaping them. But literature, I believe, is not intended solely for entertaining and consoling people. It also aims at provoking and inspiring people to read the same text twice, maybe even several times, because they want to understand it better. Thus, I think that double coding is not an aristocratic tic, but a way of showing respect for the intelligence and goodwill of the reader.

Author, Text, and Interpreters

It sometimes happens that one of my translators will ask me the following question: "I am at a loss as to how to render this passage, because it is ambiguous. It can be read two different ways. What was your intention?"

Depending on the case, I have three possible answers:

1. That's true. I have chosen the wrong expression. Please eliminate any possible misunderstanding. In the next Italian edition, I'll do the same.
2. I deliberately wanted to be ambiguous. If you read attentively, you will see that this ambiguity has a bearing on the way the text is read. Please do your best to keep the ambiguity in your rendering.
3. I did not realize that it was ambiguous, and honestly I had no intention of making it so. But as a reader I find this ambiguity very intriguing, and fruitful for the unfolding of the text. Please do your best to preserve this effect in your translation.

Now, if I had died years ago (a counterfactual conditional which has many chances to become true before the end of this century), my translator—acting as a normal reader and interpreter of my text—could have independently reached one of the following conclusions, which are in fact the same as my possible answers:

1. The ambiguity does not make any sense and complicates the reader's understanding of the text. The author probably did not realize this, so it is better to eliminate the ambiguity. "Quandoque bonus dormitat Homerus"—"Sometimes even good Homer nods."

2. It is likely that the author was being intentionally ambiguous, and I would do well to respect his decision.

3. It is possible that the author did not realize he was being ambiguous. But from a textual point of view, this effect of uncertainty is rich in connotations and innuendos that are very fruitful for the overall textual strategy.

What I would like to say here is that those who are called "creative" writers (and I explained earlier what this mischievous term can mean) should never provide interpretations of their own work. A text is a lazy machine that wants its readers to do part of its job—that is, it's a device conceived in order to elicit interpretations (as I wrote in my book *The Role of the Reader*). When one has a text to question, it is irrelevant to ask the author. At the same time, the reader cannot give just any interpretation, simply depending on his or her fancy, but must make sure that the text in some way not only legitimizes but also encourages a particular reading.

In *The Limits of Interpretation,* I distinguish between the intention of the author, the intention of the reader, and the intention of the text.

In 1962, I wrote *Opera aperta* (published in English as *The Open Work*).[1] In that book, I emphasized the active role of the interpreter in the reading of texts endowed with aesthetic value. When those pages were written, my readers mainly focused on the "open" side of the whole business, underestimating the fact that the open-ended reading I was supporting was an activity elicited by (and aimed at interpreting) the particular work. In other words, I was studying the dialectics between the rights of texts and the rights of their interpreters. I have the impression that, in the course of the past few decades, the rights of interpreters have been overstressed.

In various of my writings, I elaborated on the idea of unlimited semiosis, first formulated by C. S.

Peirce. But the notion of unlimited semiosis does not lead to the conclusion that interpretation has no criteria. For one thing, unlimited interpretation concerns systems, not processes.

Let me clarify. A linguistic system is a device from which, and by means of which, infinite linguistic strings can be produced. If we consult a dictionary for the meaning of a term, we find definitions and synonyms—that is, other words—and we look up those other words to see what they mean, so that from their definition we can switch to still other words, and so on, potentially *ad infinitum*. A dictionary is, as Joyce said of *Finnegans Wake*, a book written for an ideal reader suffering from an ideal insomnia. A good dictionary must be circular—must say what the word "cat" means by using different words; otherwise, it would be enough to close the dictionary, point at a cat, and say, "That is a cat." Very easy, and we all received this type of explanation often enough in our childhood. Yet this is not the way we know the meaning of "dinosaur," "however," "Julius Caesar," and "freedom."

In contrast, a text, insofar as it results from the manipulation of the possibilities of a system, is not open in the same way. As one composes a text, one reduces the range of possible linguistic choices. If one writes, "John is eating a . . . ," there is a strong likelihood that the following word will be a noun, and that this noun will not be "staircase" (though in certain contexts it could be "sword"). By reducing the possibility of generating infinite strings, a text also reduces the possibility of trying certain interpretations. In the lexicon of English, the pronoun "I" still means "whoever is uttering the sentence in which 'I' appears"—and therefore, according to the set of possibilities offered by the dictionary, "I" can refer to President Lincoln, Osama bin Laden, Groucho Marx, Nicole Kidman, or any one of billions of other individuals living in the present, past, or future world. But in a letter signed with my name, "I" means "Umberto Eco," irrespective of the objections that Jacques Derrida made to John Searle in the course of their famous debate on signature and context.[2]

To say that the interpretations of a text are potentially unlimited does not mean that interpretation has no object—no existing thing (whether fact or text) to focus on. To say that a text has potentially no end does not mean that every act of interpretation can have a happy end. This is why, in *The Limits of Interpretation,* I proposed a sort of criterion of falsifiability (inspired by the philosopher Karl Popper): though it may be difficult to decide whether a given interpretation is a good one, or to decide which of two interpretations of the same text is better, it is always possible to tell when a given interpretation is blatantly wrong, crazy, farfetched.

Some contemporary theories of criticism assert that the only reliable reading of a text is a misreading, and that a text exists only by virtue of the chain of responses it elicits. But this chain of responses represents the infinite *uses* we can make of a text (we could, for instance, use a Bible instead of a log as fuel in our fireplace), not the set of interpretations which depend on some acceptable conjectures about the intention of that text.

How can one prove that a conjecture about the intention of a text is acceptable? The only way is to check it against the text as a coherent whole. This idea is an old one and comes from Augustine *(De Doctrina Christiana):* any interpretation of a certain portion of a text can be accepted if it is confirmed by—and must be rejected if it is challenged by—another portion of the same text. In this sense, the internal textual coherence controls the otherwise uncontrollable drives of the reader.

Let me give an example concerning a text that intentionally and programmatically encourages the most daring interpretations—namely, *Finnegans Wake.* In the 1960s, in the journal *A Wake Newslitter,*

there was a discussion about factual historical allusions that might be identified in *Finnegans Wake*—
for instance, references to the German-Austrian
Anschluss and the Munich Pact of September 1938.[3]
In order to challenge these interpretations, Nathan
Halper pointed out that the word *Anschluss* also
has everyday nonpolitical senses (such as "connection" and "inclusion"), and that the political reading
was not supported by the context. To show how easy it
was to find just about anything in *Finnegans Wake,*
Halper took the example of Beria. First of all, at
the beginning of "The Tale of the Ondt and the
Gracehoper," he found the expression "So vi et!" and
thought it could be related to the quasi-communist
ant society. One page later, he found an allusion to
a "berial," at first glance a variant of "burial." Could
this be a reference to the Soviet minister Lavrenti
Beria? But Beria was unknown in the West before
December 9, 1938, when he was named Commissar
of Internal Affairs (prior to that, he was just a minor
functionary), and in December 1938 Joyce's manuscript was already at the printer's. Yet the word "berial" was present in a 1929 version published in *tran-
sition 12.* The question seemed to be settled on the
grounds of external proofs—though some interpreters were ready to credit Joyce with prophetic powers

and the ability to foretell Beria's rise. Ludicrous indeed—but among Joyce's fans, you can find even sillier things.

More interesting are the internal—that is, textual—proofs. In a subsequent issue of *A Wake Newslitter*, Ruth von Phul pointed out that "so vi et" could also be intended as a form of "Amen" spoken by members of authoritarian religious bodies; that the general context of those pages was not political but biblical; that the Ondt says, "As broad as Beppy's realm shall flourish my reign shall flourish!"; that "Beppy" is the Italian diminutive for "Joseph"; that "berial" could be an oblique allusion to the biblical Joseph (son of Jacob and Rachel), who was twice figuratively buried, in the pit and in prison; that Joseph begat Ephraim, who in turn begat Beriah (Chronicles 23:10); that Joseph's brother Asher had a son called Beriah (Genesis 45:30); and so on and so forth.[4]

Many of the allusions found by von Phul are no doubt farfetched, but it seems undeniable that all the references on those pages are biblical in nature. So the textual proof, too, excludes Lavrenti Beria from the Joycean opus, and Saint Augustine would have agreed.

A text is a device conceived in order to produce its Model Reader. This reader is not one who makes the "only right" conjecture. A text can foresee a Model Reader entitled to try infinite conjectures. The Empirical Reader is simply an actor who makes conjectures about the kind of Model Reader postulated by the text. Since the intention of the text is basically to produce a Model Reader who is able to make conjectures about it, the task of the Model Reader consists in figuring out a Model Author who is not the Empirical Author and who ultimately corresponds to the intention of the text.

Recognizing the intention of a text means recognizing a semiotic strategy. Sometimes the semiotic strategy is detectable on the grounds of established stylistic conventions. If a story begins with "Once upon a time," I have good reason to assume that it is a fairy tale and that the evoked and postulated Model Reader is a child (or an adult eager to react in a childlike spirit). Naturally, there might be a tone of irony, and in such a case the subsequent text should be read in a more sophisticated way. But even though one can tell, through the unfolding of the text, that this is how it should be read, the important thing to note is that the text pretended to start as a fairy tale.

When a text is sent out into the world like a message in a bottle—and this happens not only with poetry or narrative, but also with books like Kant's *Critique of Pure Reason*—that is, when a text is produced not for a single addressee but for a community of readers, the author knows that he or she will be interpreted not according to his or her intentions, but according to a complex strategy of interactions which also involves the readers, along with their competence in their language as a social treasury. By "social treasury" I mean not only a given language comprising a set of grammatical rules, but also the whole encyclopedia that the performances of the language have generated: the cultural conventions that this language has produced and the history of the previous interpretations of its many texts, including the text that the reader is in the course of reading.

The act of reading must take into account all of these elements, even though it is unlikely that a single reader can master them all. Thus, every act of reading is a complex transaction between the competence of the reader (the reader's world knowledge) and the kind of competence that a given text postulates in order to be read in an "economical" way—meaning a way that increases the comprehension and enjoyment of the text, and that is supported by the context.

The Model Reader of a story is not the Empirical Reader. The Empirical Reader is you, me, anyone, when we read a text. Empirical Readers can read in many ways, and there is no law that tells them how to read, because they often use the text as a vehicle for their own passions, which may come from outside the text or which the text may arouse by chance.

Let me describe some funny situations in which one of my readers acted as an Empirical Reader, rather than as a Model Reader. A childhood friend of mine whom I hadn't seen for years wrote to me after the publication of my second novel, *Foucault's Pendulum:* "Dear Umberto, I do not recall having told you the pathetic story of my uncle and aunt, but I think you were very indiscreet to use it in your novel." Well, in my book I recount a few episodes concerning a certain Uncle Charles and Aunt Catherine, who in the story are the uncle and aunt of the protagonist, Jacopo Belbo. It is true that such people really did exist. With a few alterations, I was telling a story from my childhood concerning an uncle and aunt of mine—but they of course had different names from those of the characters. I answered my friend saying that Uncle Charles and Aunt Catherine were *my* relations, not his own (therefore I held the copyright), and that I was not even aware he had an uncle or aunt. My friend apologized: he had been so absorbed by the story that he thought he'd recognized some incidents that had happened to his uncle and aunt—which is not impossible, because in wartime (the period to which my memories went back) similar things can happen to different uncles and aunts.

What had happened to my friend? He had sought in my story something that was instead in his personal memory. He was not interpreting my text, but rather *using* it. It is hardly forbidden to use a text for daydreaming, and we all do so frequently—but this is not a public affair. Using a text in this way means moving within it as if it were our own private journal.

There are certain rules of the game, and the Model Reader is someone eager to play such a game. My friend forgot the name of the game and superimposed his own expectations as Empirical Reader on the expectations that the author wanted from a Model Reader.

In Chapter 115 of *Foucault's Pendulum,* my hero, Casaubon, on the night of June 23–24, 1984, having attended an occultist ceremony at the Conservatoire des Arts et Métiers in Paris, walks, as if possessed, the entire length of the Rue Saint-Martin, crosses the Rue aux Ours, arrives at the Centre Beaubourg, and then comes to Saint-Merry Church. Afterward he continues along various streets, all of them named in my book, until he gets to the Place des Vosges.

As I said earlier, in order to write that chapter I

followed the same route for several nights, carrying a tape recorder, taking notes on what I could see and the impressions I had (I am revealing my methods here, as Empirical Author). Moreover, since I had a computer program which showed me what the sky looks like at any time, in any year, at whatever longitude or latitude, I even found out that there had been a moon that night, and that it could have been seen from specific locations at various times. I did this not because I wanted to emulate Emile Zola's realism, but (as I have said) because I like to have the scene I'm writing about in front of me while I narrate.

After publishing the novel, I received a letter from a man who had evidently gone to the National Library to read all the newspapers from June 24, 1984. And he had discovered that on the corner of the Rue Réaumur—which I hadn't actually named, but which does cross the Rue Saint-Martin at a certain point—after midnight, more or less at the time Casaubon passed by, there had been a fire, and a big fire at that, since it had been mentioned in the papers. The reader asked me how Casaubon had managed not to see it.

I answered that Casaubon had certainly seen the fire, but that he hadn't mentioned it for some mysterious reason, unknown to me—which was pretty likely in a story so thick with mysteries both true and false. My reader is no doubt still trying to find out why Casaubon kept silent about that fire, suspecting another conspiracy by the Knights Templar. The truth is that I probably did not pass by that corner at midnight, but came to it just before the fire broke out or shortly after it was extinguished. I do not know. I only know that my reader was using my text for his own purposes: he wanted it to correspond, in every detail, to what had happened in the real world.

Now let me tell you another story concerning the same night. The difference is that, in the case I just mentioned, a fussy reader wanted my story to correspond to the real world, whereas in the following instance, readers wanted the real world to correspond to my fiction—a case that is a little different and more rewarding.

Two students from the Ecole des Beaux-Arts in Paris came to show me a photo album in which they had reconstructed the entire route taken by Casaubon. They had found and photographed all of the places I had mentioned, one by one, at the same time of night. At the end of Chapter 115, Casaubon comes up out of the city drains and enters, through the cellar, an Asian bar full of sweating customers, beer kegs, and greasy spits. The students actually found that bar and took a photo of it. It goes without saying that the bar was an invention of mine, though I designed it thinking of the many pubs in that neighborhood; but those two boys had undoubtedly discovered the bar described in my book. I repeat: those students had not superimposed on their duty as Model Readers the concern of the Empirical Reader who wants to check and see if my novel described the real Paris. Rather, they wanted to transform the "real" Paris into a place that existed in my book. In fact, of all that they could have found in Paris, they chose only those aspects that corresponded to the descriptions provided by my text.

That bar existed in my text, even though I believed I had simply imagined it. In the face of its presence in the text, the intention of the Empirical Author becomes rather irrelevant. Authors frequently say things they are unaware of; only after they have gotten the reactions of their readers do they discover what they have said.

There is, however, a case in which it can be enlightening to look at the intentions of the Empirical Author. It is when the author is still living, the critics have offered their interpretations of the text, and one can ask the author to what extent he or she, as an empirical person, was aware of the manifold interpretations that the text supported. At this point, the author's response should be used not in order to validate the interpretations of the text, but in order to show the discrepancies between his or her intention and the intention of the text. The aim of the experiment is theoretical, rather than critical.

Finally, there is the case in which the author is also a textual theorist. In this instance, the author might respond in two different ways. The response could be: "I did not mean this, but I must agree that the text says it, and I thank the reader for making me aware of it." Or it could be: "Independently of the fact that I did not mean this, I think that a reasonable reader should not accept such an interpretation, because it is uneconomical."

Now let me describe some cases in which, as an Empirical Author, I had to surrender in the face of a reader who was sticking to the intention of my text.

In *Reflections on "The Name of the Rose,"* I said I felt a thrill of satisfaction when I read a review that quoted a remark made by William at the end of the trial, in the chapter "Fifth Day, Nones." "What terrifies you most in purity?" Adso asks. And William answers: "Haste." I loved, and still love, these two lines very much. But then one of my readers pointed out to me that on the same page, Bernard Gui, threatening the cellarer with torture, says: "Justice is not inspired by haste, as the Pseudo-Apostles believe, and the justice of God has centuries at its disposal." The reader rightly asked me what connection I had meant to establish between the haste feared by William and the absence of haste extolled by Bernard. I was unable to answer.

As a matter of fact, the exchange between Adso and William does not exist in the original manuscript; I added this brief dialogue in the galleys, because for reasons of balance and rhythm I needed to insert another few lines before giving Bernard the floor again. And I completely forgot that, a bit later, Bernard speaks of haste. He uses a stereotyped expression, the sort of thing we would expect from a judge—a commonplace on the order of, "All are equal before the law." Alas, when juxtaposed with the haste mentioned by William, the haste mentioned by Bernard gives the impression that he is saying something substantive instead of formulaic; and the reader is justified in wondering whether the two men are saying the same thing, or whether the loathing of haste expressed by William is not imperceptibly different from the loathing of haste expressed by Bernard. The text is there, and produces its own effects. Whether I wanted it this way or not, we are now faced with a question, a provocative ambiguity—and I myself am at a loss as to how to resolve this conflict, though I realize a meaning lurks there (perhaps even many meanings).

An author who has entitled his book *The Name of the Rose* must be ready to encounter manifold interpretations of his title. As an Empirical Author, I wrote (in *Reflections*) that I had chosen that title precisely in order to set the reader free: "The rose is a figure so rich in meanings that by now it hardly has any meaning left: Dante's mystic rose, and 'Go, lovely Rose,' the Wars of the Roses, 'Rose thou art sick,' too many rings around the rosie, 'a rose by any other name,' 'a rose is a rose is a rose is a rose,' the Rosicrucians . . ." Moreover, a scholar has discovered that some early manuscripts of *De Contemptu Mundi*, by Bernard de Morlay—from which I borrowed the hexameter that closes my novel: "Stat rosa pristina nomine, nomina nuda tenemus" ("The rose of yesteryear survives only in its name; names alone are all that we have")—read "Stat *Roma* pristina nomine," which after all seems more consistent with the rest of the poem and its allusions to the lost Babylon.[5] So the title of my novel, had I come across another version of Morlay's poem, could have been *The Name of Rome* (and would have acquired fascist overtones).

But the title is actually *The Name of the Rose*, and

I understand now how difficult it was to curtail the infinite series of connotations that the word "rose" elicits. I may have intended to multiply the possible readings to such an extent that any one of them would become irrelevant, and as a result I produced a vast and inescapable series of interpretations. But the text is out there in the world, and the Empirical Author has to remain silent.

When I named one of the main characters in *Foucault's Pendulum* "Casaubon," I was thinking of Isaac Casaubon, who in 1614 demonstrated that the *Corpus Hermeticum* was a forgery; and if one reads *Foucault's Pendulum,* one can find some parallels between what the great philologist understood and what my character finally understands. I was aware that few readers would get the allusion, but I was equally aware that, in terms of textual strategy, such knowledge was not indispensable. (I mean that one can read my novel and understand my Casaubon even without knowing anything about the historical Casaubon. Many authors like to put certain shibboleths into their texts, for the benefit of a few experienced readers.) Before finishing my novel, I discovered by chance that Casaubon was also a character in George Eliot's *Middlemarch,* a novel I had read decades before but forgotten about. This was a case in which, as a Model Author, I tried to eliminate a possible reference to George Eliot. In Chapter 10, the English translation contains the following exchange between Belbo and Casaubon:

> "By the way, what's your name?"
> "Casaubon."
> "Casaubon. Wasn't he a character in *Middlemarch?*"
> "I don't know. There was also a Renaissance philologist by that name, but we are not related."

I did my best to avoid what I considered a useless reference to Mary Ann Evans. But then a smart reader, David Robey, remarked that Eliot's Casaubon was writing a book entitled *Key to All Mythologies.* As a Model Reader, I felt obliged to accept that association. The text plus encyclopedic knowledge entitles any cultivated reader to find that connection. It makes sense. Too bad for the Empirical Author who is not as smart as his readers.

In the same vein, my novel is entitled *Foucault's Pendulum* because the pendulum it speaks of was invented by Léon Foucault. If the device had been invented by Ben Franklin, the title would have been *Franklin's Pendulum.* This time, I was aware from the very beginning that somebody might smell an allusion to Michel Foucault: my characters are obsessed by analogies, and Foucault wrote on the paradigm of similarity. As an Empirical Author, I was not happy with such a possible connection. It sounds like a joke, and not a clever one. But the pendulum invented by Léon was the hero of my story and determined the title; so I hoped that my Model Reader would not try to make a superficial connection with Michel. I was wrong—many smart readers did so. The text is there. Maybe they are right; maybe I am responsible for a superficial joke; maybe the joke is not that superficial. I do not know. By now, the whole affair is out of my control.

Now let's consider cases in which—though I may have forgotten my initial intentions, while acting as a Model Reader and checking the text—I think I have the right, like every other human being, to refuse interpretations that do not seem economical.

Helena Costiucovich, before translating into Russian (masterfully) *The Name of the Rose,* wrote a long essay on it.[6] At a certain point, she mentions a book by Emile Henriot entitled *La Rose de Bratislava* (1946), which deals with the hunt for a mysterious manuscript and concludes with the destruction of a library by fire. The story takes place in Prague, and at the beginning of my novel I mention Prague. Moreover, one of my librarians is named Berengar and one of the librarians in Henriot's book is named Berngard.

I had never read Henriot's novel, and was unaware that it existed. I have read interpretations in which my critics turned up sources that I knew about, and I was very happy that they so cunningly discovered what I had so cunningly concealed in order to lead them to find it—for instance, the fact that Serenus Zeitblom and Adrian Leverkühn in Thomas Mann's *Doctor Faustus* were the model for the narrative relationship between Adso and William in *The Name of the Rose*. Readers have informed me about sources I'd never heard of, and I was delighted to be thought sufficiently erudite to quote them (recently a young medievalist told me that a blind librarian was mentioned by Cassiodorus in the sixth century A.D.). I have read critical analyses in which the interpreter discovered influences that I didn't think of when I was writing but that I had certainly read in my youth; clearly, I had been unconsciously influenced by them. My friend Giorgio Celli, for example, said that my long-ago readings must have included the novels of the Symbolist writer Dmitry Merezhkovsky, and I realized he was right.

As an ordinary reader of *The Name of the Rose*

(leaving aside the fact that I'm the author), I think that Helena Costiucovich's argument does not prove anything interesting. The quest for a mysterious manuscript and the destruction of a library by fire are very common literary topoi, and I could cite many other books that use them. Prague is mentioned at the beginning of the novel, but if instead of Prague I had mentioned Budapest, it would have been the same. Prague does not play a crucial role in the story.

By the way, when *The Name of the Rose* was translated in a certain Eastern-bloc country, long before perestroika, the translator called me and said that the novel's opening reference to Russia's invasion of Czechoslovakia could cause problems. I answered that I did not approve any changes in my text, and that if it was censored in any way I would hold the publisher responsible. Then, as a joke, I added: "I mention Prague at the beginning because it is one of my magical cities. But I also like Dublin. Insert 'Dublin' instead of 'Prague.' It does not make any difference." The translator protested, "But Dublin was not invaded by Russians!" I replied, "That is not my fault."

Finally, the names "Berengar" and "Berngard" could be a coincidence. In any case, the Model

Reader must admit that the four coincidences—manuscript, fire, Prague, and Berengar—are interesting. And as an Empirical Author, I have no right to object. Notwithstanding all this, I recently came across a copy of the French text by Henriot, and I discovered that the name of the librarian in his book is not Berngard, but Bernhard—Bernhard Marr. Costiucovich probably relied on a Russian edition in which the name was badly transliterated into Cyrillic. Thus, at least one of the curious coincidences is eliminated, and my Model Reader can relax a little.

But Helena Costiucovich wrote something more to establish the parallels between my book and Henriot's. She said that in Henriot's novel, the coveted manuscript was the original copy of Casanova's memoirs. It so happens that in my novel there is a minor character called Hugh of Newcastle (in the Italian version, Ugo di Novocastro). Costiucovich's conclusion is that "only by passing from one name to another is it possible to conceive of the name of the rose."

As an Empirical Author, I could say that Hugh of Newcastle is not an invention of mine, but a historical figure mentioned in the medieval sources I used: the episode of the meeting between the Franciscan legation and the papal representatives is actually derived from a fourteenth-century chronicle. But the reader cannot be expected to know this, and my re-action cannot be taken into account. Yet I think I do have the right to state my opinion as an ordinary reader. First of all, "Newcastle" is not a translation of "Casanova," which should be translated as "New House" (etymologically speaking, the meaning of the Latin name "Novocastro" is "New City" or "New Encampment"). Thus, "Newcastle" suggests "Casa-nova" the same way it could suggest "Newton."

But there are other elements which can textually prove that Costiucovich's hypothesis is uneconomi-cal. First of all, Hugh of Newcastle shows up in the novel playing a very marginal role, and has nothing to do with the library. If the text wanted to suggest a pertinent relationship between Hugh and the li-brary (as well as between him and the manuscript), it should have said something more. But the text does not say a word about that. Second, Casanova was—at least according to culturally shared, encyclopedic knowledge—a professional lover and a rake, whereas nothing in the novel casts doubt on the virtue of Hugh. Third, there is no evident connection between a manuscript by Casanova and a manuscript by Ar-istotle, and the novel nowhere alludes to libertin-age as a praiseworthy form of behavior. As a Model

Reader of my own novel, I feel entitled to say that looking for a "Casanova connection" does not lead anywhere.

Once, during a debate, a reader asked me what I meant by the sentence, "The supreme happiness lies in having what you have." I was disconcerted, and declared that I had never written that sentence. I was sure of it, and for many reasons. First, I do not think that happiness lies in having what one has; not even Snoopy would subscribe to such a banality. Second, a medieval character is unlikely to think that happiness lies in having what he actually has, since, in the medieval mind, happiness was a future state to be attained through present suffering. Thus, I repeated that I had never written that line, and my interlocutor looked at me as if I were unable to recognize what I myself had written.

Later, I came across that quotation. It appears in *The Name of the Rose*, during the description of Adso's erotic ecstasy in the kitchen. This episode, as the dullest of my readers can easily guess, is entirely made up of quotations from the Song of Songs and from medieval mystics. In any case, even though the sources are not identified, the reader can tell that these pages depict the feelings of a young man after his first (and probably last) sexual experience. If one rereads the line in context (I mean the context of the novel, not necessarily the context of the medieval sources), one finds: "O Lord, when the soul is transported, the only virtue lies in having what you see; the supreme happiness is having what you have." Thus, "happiness lies in having what you have" not in general, at every moment of your life, but only at the moment of the ecstatic vision. This is a case in which it is unnecessary to know the intention of the Empirical Author: the intention of the text is blatant. And if English words have a conventional meaning, the actual sense of the text is not the sense which that reader—obeying some idiosyncratic urge—believed that it wanted to convey. Between the unattainable intention of the author and the arguable intention of the reader, there is the transparent intention of the text, which refutes untenable interpretations.

I enjoyed reading a beautiful book by Robert F. Fleissner, *A Rose by Another Name: A Survey of Literary Flora from Shakespeare to Eco*—and I hope Shakespeare would have been proud to find his name associated with mine. As Fleissner discusses the various connections he has found between my rose and all the other roses of world literature, he says something quite interesting: he wishes to show "how Eco's rose derived from Doyle's 'Adventure of the Naval Treaty,' which, in turn, owed much to Cuff's admiration of this flower in *The Moonstone*."[7]

Now, I am a thorough Wilkie Collins addict, but I do not remember (and certainly did not when writing my novel) that the character of Cuff has a passion for roses. I think I have read everything Arthur Conan Doyle ever wrote, but I must confess I do not remember "The Adventure of the Naval Treaty." This does not matter: in my novel, there are so many explicit references to Sherlock Holmes that my text can support this connection as well. But in spite of my openmindedness, I think Fleissner is overinterpreting when, trying to demonstrate how much my William "echoes" Holmes's admiration for roses, he quotes this passage from my book: "'Frangula,' William said suddenly, bending over to observe a plant that, on that winter day, he recognized from the bare bush. 'A good infusion is made from the bark.'"

It is curious that Fleissner stops his quotation after "bark." After a comma, my text continues with the phrase: "for hemorrhoids." Honestly, I think that the Model Reader is not invited to take "frangula" as an allusion to roses.

Giosue Musca wrote a critical analysis of *Foucault's Pendulum* that I consider among the best I have read.[8] Yet from the outset, he admits having been corrupted by the analogy-seeking habit of my characters and goes fishing for connections. He masterfully points out many ultraviolet quotations and stylistic analogies I wanted to be discovered; he finds other connections I did not think of but that sound very persuasive; and he plays the role of a paranoiac reader by spotting connections that amaze me but that I am unable to disprove—even though I know they can mislead the reader. For instance, it seems that the name of the computer, Abulafia, plus the names of the three main characters, Belbo, Casaubon, and Diotallevi, yields the initials ABCD. Useless to say that right up until I completed the manuscript, the computer had a different name: readers could object that I unconsciously changed it simply in order to obtain an alphabetic series. It seems that Jacopo Belbo is fond of whisky and his initials are, oddly enough, JB. Useless to protest that throughout the writing process, his first name was not Jacopo but Stefano, and that I changed it to Jacopo at the last moment. There is no allusion to J&B whisky.

The only objections I can make as a Model Reader of my book are (1) that the alphabetic series ABCD is textually irrelevant if the names of the other characters do not extend the string to X, Y, and Z; (2) that Belbo also drinks martinis and, furthermore, his mild alcoholic addiction is not his most significant feature.

In contrast, I cannot argue with my reader when he also notes that Cesare Pavese, a writer whom I loved and still love very much, was born in a village called Santo Stefano Belbo and that my Belbo, a melancholic Piedmontese, remembers Pavese. As a matter of fact (though my Model Reader is not supposed to know this detail), I spent my childhood on the banks of the River Belbo, where I underwent some of the ordeals that I attributed to Jacopo Belbo. It is true that all this happened a long time before I learned about Cesare Pavese, so that I changed the original name of Stefano Belbo to Jacopo Belbo precisely to avoid making a blatant connection with Pavese. But this was not enough, and my reader was right in finding a connection between Pavese and Jacopo Belbo. Probably he would be right even if I had called Belbo by any other name.

I could keep going with examples of this sort, but I have chosen to mention only those that were more immediately comprehensible. I have skipped other, more complex cases because I risked going too deeply into matters of philosophical or aesthetic interpretation. I hope you will agree that I have introduced the Empirical Author in this game only in order to stress his irrelevance and to reassert the rights of the text.

As I near the end of my remarks, however, I feel that I have been scarcely generous to the Empirical Author. There is at least one case in which the testimony of the Empirical Author fulfills an important function: not so much to enable readers to better understand his texts, but certainly to help them understand the unpredictable course of every creative process. Understanding the creative process also means understanding how certain textual solutions come about by serendipity, or as the result of unconscious mechanisms. This helps us to understand the difference between the strategy of the text—a linguistic object that Model Readers have before their eyes, enabling them to make judgments independently of the Empirical Author's intentions—and the story of the evolution of that text.

Some of the examples I have given can work in this direction. Let me now add two other curious examples, which have a special feature: they concern only my personal life and do not have any detectable textual counterpart. They are irrelevant to the business of interpretation. They simply tell how a text, which is a machine conceived in order to elicit interpretations, sometimes grows out of a deep-flowing magma which has nothing—or nothing yet—to do with literature.

First story. In *Foucault's Pendulum,* the young Casaubon is in love with a Brazilian girl called Amparo. Giosue Musca found, tongue in cheek, a connection with the physicist André-Marie Ampère, who studied the magnetic force between electrical currents. Too smart. I did not know why I had chosen that name. I realized it was not a Brazilian name, so I decided to write (in Chapter 23): "I never did understand how it was that Amparo, a descendant of Dutch settlers in Recife who intermarried with Indians and Sudanese blacks—with her Jamaican face and Parisian culture—had wound up with a Spanish name." In other words, I chose the name "Amparo" as if it came from outside my novel.

Months after the publication of the book, a friend asked me: "Why 'Amparo'? Isn't that the name of a mountain, or of a girl who looks at a mountain?" And then he explained: "There is a song, 'Guajira Guantanamera,' which mentions something like 'Amparo.'" Oh, my God. I knew that song very well, even though I did not remember a single word of it. It was sung, in the mid-1950s, by a girl I was in love with at the time. She was Latin American, and very beautiful. She was not Brazilian, not Marxist, not black, not hysterical, as Amparo is; but it is clear that, when inventing a charming Latin American girl, I unconsciously thought of that other image from my youth, when I was Casaubon's age. I had thought of that song, and in some way the name "Amparo," which I had completely forgotten, had migrated from my unconscious to the page. This story is completely irrelevant to the interpretation of the novel. Insofar as the text is concerned, Amparo is Amparo is Amparo is Amparo.

Second story. Those who have read *The Name of the Rose* know that it concerns a mysterious manuscript, that this lost work is the second book of Aristotle's *Poetics*, that its pages are smeared with poison, and that it is described (in the chapter "Seventh Day, Night") like this: "He read the first page aloud, then stopped, as if he were not interested in knowing more, and rapidly leafed through the following pages. But after a few pages he encountered resistance, because near the upper corner of the side edge, and along the top, some pages had stuck together, as happens when the damp and deteriorating papery substance forms a kind of sticky paste."

I wrote those lines at the end of 1979. In the following years, perhaps because after publishing *The Name of the Rose* I started to be more frequently in touch with librarians and book collectors (and certainly because I had a little more money at my disposal), I became a rare-book collector. It had happened before, in the course of my life, that I had bought some old books, but I had done so by chance, and just when they were very cheap. Only in the past twenty-five years have I become a serious book collector—and "serious" means that one has to consult specialized catalogues and must write, for every book, a technical file, including the collation, historical information on the previous or subsequent editions, and a precise description of the physical state of one's copy. This last job requires technical jargon, for specifying whether the book is foxed, browned, water-stained, or soiled, and whether it has washed or crisp leaves, cropped margins, erasures, rebaked bindings, rubbed joints, and so on.

One day, rummaging through the upper shelves of my home library, I discovered a copy of Aristotle's *Poetics,* annotated by Antonio Riccoboni, Padua, 1587. I had completely forgotten about it. The numeral 1,000 was written in pencil on the endpaper, meaning that I had bought the book somewhere for a thousand lire (today, roughly seventy U.S. cents), probably in the 1950s. My catalogues said that it was a second edition, not exceedingly rare, and that there was a copy of it in the British Museum. But I was happy to have it because apparently it was difficult to find, and in any case the commentary by Riccoboni was less widely known and less frequently quoted than, say, those by Robortello or Castelvetro.

So I started writing my description. I copied the title page and discovered that the edition had an appendix entitled, "Ejusdem Ars Comica ex Aristotele," claiming to present Aristotle's lost book on comedy. Evidently, Riccoboni had tried to reconstruct the lost second book of the *Poetics*. This was not, however, an unusual endeavor, and I went on to complete the physical description of the volume. Then I had an experience similar to that of a certain Zasetsky, described by the Soviet neuro-psychologist A. R. Luria.[9] Zasetsky had lost part of his brain during World War II, and with it the whole of his memory and his speaking ability—yet he was nevertheless still able to write. His hand automatically wrote down all the information he was unable to think of, and step by step he reconstructed his own identity by reading what he had written.

Likewise, I was looking coldly and technically at the book, writing my description, and suddenly I realized that I was rewriting *The Name of the Rose*. The only difference was that from page 120, when the *Ars Comica* begins, the lower rather than the upper margins were severely damaged—but all the rest was the same. The pages, progressively browned and damp-stained, stuck together at the edges and looked as if they were smeared with a disgusting greasy substance.

I was holding in my hands, in printed form, the manuscript I had described in my novel. I had had it for years and years in my home, right on my shelf.

It was not an extraordinary coincidence, or even a miracle. I had bought the book in my youth, skimmed through it, realized it was badly soiled, put it away somewhere, and forgotten about it. But using a sort of internal camera, I had photographed those pages, and for decades the image of those poisonous leaves had lain in the most remote part of my soul, as if in a grave, until the moment it reemerged—I do not know why—and I believed I had invented the book.

This story, like the first, has nothing to do with a possible interpretation of *The Name of the Rose*. The moral, if it has any, is that the private life of Empirical Authors is, to a certain extent, even more unfathomable than their texts. Between the mysterious history of a textual creation and the uncontrollable drift of its future readings, the text *qua* text still represents a comforting presence, a point to which we can hold fast.

3

Some Remarks on Fictional Characters

[Don Quixote] became so absorbed in his books that he
spent his nights from sunset to sunrise, and his days from
dawn to dusk, poring over them; and what with little sleep
and much reading, his brains got so dry that he lost his
wits. His fancy grew full of what he used to read about
in his books — enchantments, quarrels, battles, challenges,
wounds, wooings, loves, agonies, and all sorts of impossible nonsense; and it so possessed his mind that the
whole fabric of invention and fancy he read of was true,
that to him no history in the world had more reality in it. He
used to say the Cid Ruy Díaz was a very good knight, but
that he was not to be compared with the Knight of the
Burning Sword, who with one back-stroke cut in half two
fierce and monstrous giants. He thought more of Bernardo
del Carpio, because at Roncesvalles he slew Roland in spite
of enchantments.

— Cervantes, *Don Quixote*, trans. John Ormsby

After the publication of *The Name of the Rose*, many
readers wrote to me saying that they had discovered
and visited the abbey where I set my story. Many
others asked for more information about the manuscript I mention in the book's introduction. In the

same introduction, I say that I found an unnamed book by Athanasius Kircher at an antiquarian bookshop in Buenos Aires. Recently—that is, nearly thirty years after the publication of my novel—a German fellow wrote to me saying that he had just found an antiquarian bookshop in Buenos Aires with a volume by Kircher, and he wondered if by chance they were the same shop and the same book I mention in my novel.

It is useless to say that I invented both the layout and the location of the abbey (though many of its details were inspired by real sites); that beginning a fictional work by saying that one has found an old manuscript is a venerable literary topos, to such an extent that I entitled my introduction "*Naturally,* a Manuscript"; and that the mysterious book by Kircher and the even more mysterious antiquarian shop were both invented.

Now, those who looked for the real abbey and the real manuscript were perhaps naive readers unfamiliar with literary conventions, who stumbled on my novel by accident after seeing the movie. But the German fellow I just mentioned, who seems in the habit of visiting rare-book dealers and who apparently knows about Kircher, is certainly a cultivated person, familiar with books and printed materials. Thus, it seems that a lot of readers, regardless of their cultural status, are, or become, unable to distinguish between fiction and reality. They take fictional characters seriously, as if the characters were real human beings.

Another comment on this distinction (or the lack of it) occurs in *Foucault's Pendulum*. Jacopo Belbo, after attending a dreamlike alchemical liturgy, tries to ironically justify the practice of the worshipers by observing: "The question isn't whether these people here are better or worse than Christians who go to shrines. I was asking myself: Who do we think we are? We for whom Hamlet is more real than our janitor? Do I have any right to judge—I who keep searching for my own Madame Bovary so we can have a big scene?"[1]

Weeping for Anna Karenina

In 1860, on the verge of sailing through the Mediterranean to follow Garibaldi's expedition to Sicily, Alexandre Dumas *père* stopped in Marseille and visited the Château d'If, where his hero, Edmond Dantès, before becoming the Count of Monte Cristo, was imprisoned for fourteen years and was tutored in his cell by a fellow inmate, the abbé Faria.[2] While Dumas was there, he discovered that visitors were regularly shown what was called the "real" cell of Monte Cristo, and that the guides constantly spoke of Dantès, Faria, and the other characters of the novel as if they had really existed.[3] In contrast, the same guides never mentioned that the Château d'If had held as prisoners some important historical figures, such as Honoré Mirabeau.

Thus, Dumas comments in his memoirs: "It is the privilege of novelists to create characters who kill those of the historians. The reason is that historians evoke mere ghosts, while novelists create flesh-and-blood people."[4]

Once a friend of mine urged me to organize a symposium on the following subject: If we know that Anna Karenina is a fictional character who does not exist in the real world, why do we weep over her plight, or at any rate why are we deeply moved by her misfortunes?

There are probably many highly educated readers who do not shed tears over the fate of Scarlett O'Hara but are nevertheless shocked by the fate of Anna Karenina. Moreover, I have seen sophisticated intellectuals openly weep at the end of *Cyrano de Bergerac*—a fact that should not astonish anybody, because when a dramatic strategy aims at inducing the audience to shed tears, it makes them weep regardless of their cultural level. This is not an aesthetic problem: great works of art may not evoke an emotional response, whereas many bad films and dime novels succeed in doing so.[5] And let's remember that Madame Bovary, a character for whom many readers have wept, used to cry over the love stories she was reading.

I told my friend firmly that this phenomenon had neither ontological nor logical relevance, and could be of interest only to psychologists. We can identify with fictional characters and with their deeds because, according to a narrative agreement, we start living in the possible world of their story as if it were our own real world. But this does not occur only when we read fiction.

Many of us have sometimes thought of the possible death of a loved one and have been deeply affected, if not moved to tears, even though we knew that the event was imagined and not real. Such phenomena of identification and projection are absolutely normal and (I repeat) are a matter for psychologists. If there are optical illusions, in which we see a given form as bigger than another even though we know they are exactly the same size, why shouldn't there be emotional illusions as well?[6]

I also tried to show my friend that the capacity of a fictional character to make people cry depends not only on his or her qualities but on the cultural habits of the readers—or on the relationship between their cultural expectations and the narrative strategy. In the mid-nineteenth century people cried, even sobbed, over the fate of Eugène Sue's Fleur-de-Marie, while today the misfortunes of the poor girl leave us cynically unmoved. In contrast, decades ago a lot of people were moved by the fate of Jenny in Erich Segal's *Love Story*, both the novel and the film.

Eventually, I came to realize that I could not so easily dismiss the whole question. I had to admit that there is a difference between weeping at the imagined death of a loved one and weeping over the death of Anna Karenina. It is true that in both cases we are taking for granted what happens in a possible world: the world of our imagination in the first case, and a world designed by Tolstoy in the second case. But if later we are asked if our loved one has really passed away, we can say with great relief that it is not true—the way we are relieved when we awake from a nightmare. Whereas if we are asked whether Anna Karenina has died, we must always answer yes, since the fact that Anna committed suicide is true in all possible worlds.

Moreover, when it comes to romantic love, we suffer when we imagine being abandoned by our beloved, and some people who have actually been abandoned are driven to suicide. But we do not suffer too much if our friends are abandoned by their beloved. We certainly sympathize with them, but I have never heard of anyone who committed suicide because one of his friends had been abandoned. It thus seems strange that, when Goethe published *Die Leiden des jungen Werthers* (The Sorrows of Young Werther), in which the hero, Werther, commits suicide because of his ill-fated love, many romantic young readers did the same. The phenomenon came to be known as the "Werther effect." What does it mean when people are only slightly disturbed by the death from starvation of millions of real individuals—including many children—but they feel great personal anguish at the death of Anna Karenina? What does it mean when we deeply share the sorrow of a person who we know has never existed?

Ontology versus Semiotics

But are we sure that fictional characters do not have some kind of existence? Let us use the term "Physically Existing Object," or PhEO, for objects that currently exist (like you and the moon and the city of Atlanta), as well as for objects that existed only in the past (like Julius Caesar or Columbus's ships).

Certainly nobody would say that fictional characters are PhEOs. But this does not mean that they are not objects at all.

It suffices to adopt the sort of ontology developed by Alexius Meinong (1853–1920) to accept the idea that every representation or judgment must correspond to an object, even though the object may not necessarily be an existing one. An object is anything endowed with certain properties, but existence is not an indispensable property. Seven centuries before Meinong, the philosopher Avicenna said that existence was merely an accidental property of an essence or substance ("accidens adveniens quidditati"). In this sense, there can be *abstract* objects—like the number seventeen and a right angle, which do not properly exist but *subsist*—and *concrete* objects, like myself and Anna Karenina, with the difference that I am a PhEO and Anna is not.

Now, I wish to make clear that I am not concerned here with the ontology of fictional characters. To become the subject of ontological reflection, an object must be considered as existing independent of any mind, as is the case with a right angle, which many mathematicians and philosophers view as a sort of Platonic entity—meaning that the assertion "The right angle has ninety degrees" would remain true even if our species disappeared, and its truth would also be accepted by aliens from outer space.

In contrast, the fact that Anna Karenina committed suicide depends on the cultural competence of many living readers; it is attested to by some books, but it would certainly be forgotten if the human species and all the books on this planet disappeared. A possible objection is that a right angle will have ninety degrees only for aliens who share our Euclidean geometry, and that every assertion about Anna Karenina would remain true also for aliens if they succeeded in retrieving at least one copy of Tolstoy's novel. But I am not obliged here to adopt a stance on the Platonic nature of mathematical entities, and I do not have any information about the geometry or the comparative literature of aliens. Let me assume, at any rate, that the Pythagorean theorem would probably be true even if no humans existed to think of it, whereas if some existence is to be attributed to Anna Karenina, there certainly needs to be a quasi-human mind that is able to transform Tolstoy's text into mental phenomena.

The only thing I am pretty sure of is that some people are moved by the revelation that Anna Karenina committed suicide, but very few (if any) are shocked or saddened when they learn that a right angle has ninety degrees. Since the core of my reflections here is why people are moved by fictional characters, I cannot assume an ontological point of view. I am obliged to consider Anna Karenina as a mind-dependent object, an object of cognition. In other words (and I shall explain my point of view more clearly below), my approach is not ontological but semiotic. That is, my concern is what sort of content corresponds, for a competent reader, to the expression "Anna Karenina"—especially if that reader takes it for granted that Anna is not and has never been a PhEO.[7]

Moreover, the problem I am investigating is: In what sense can a normal reader take as true the assertion "Anna Karenina committed suicide," if he or she knows for sure that Anna is not a PhEO? The question I am asking is not "Where, in which region of the universe, do fictional characters live?" but rather, "In what way do we speak about them as if they lived in some region of the universe?"

To answer, if possible, all these questions, I think it will be useful to reconsider some obvious facts about fictional characters and the world they live in.

Incomplete Possible Worlds and Complete Characters

By definition, fictional texts clearly speak of non-existent persons and events (and precisely for this reason, they call for the suspension of our disbelief). Therefore, from the point of view of a truth-conditional semantics, a fictional assertion always states something that is contrary to fact.

Nevertheless, we do not take fictional assertions as lies. First of all, when reading a piece of fiction, we enter into a tacit agreement with its author, who *pretends* that what he or she has written is true and asks us to *pretend* to take it seriously.[8] In so doing, every novelist designs a possible world, and all our judgments of truth and falsehood relate to that possible world. Thus, it is fictionally true that Sherlock Holmes lived on Baker Street and fictionally false that he lived on the banks of the Spoon River.

Fictional texts never take as their setting a world which is totally different from the one we live in, not even if they are fairy tales or science fiction stories. Even in such situations, if a forest is mentioned, it is understood that it should be more or less like the forests of our real world, where the trees are vegetal and not mineral, and so on. If by chance we are told that the forest consists of mineral trees, the notions of "mineral" and "tree" should be the same as in our real world.

Usually a novel chooses as its setting the world of our everyday life, at least insofar as its main features are concerned. The stories of Rex Stout ask their readers to take as true the fact that New York City is inhabited by people such as Nero Wolfe, Archie Goodwin, Saul Panzer, and Inspector Cramer, who are not listed in the records of the New York municipal registry. But all the rest of the action occurs in a New York which is as it is (or was) in our real world, so that we would be disconcerted if suddenly Archie Goodwin decided to climb the Eiffel Tower in Central Park. A fictional world is not only a *possible world* but also a *small world*—that is, "a relatively short course of local events in some nook or corner of the actual world."[9]

A fictional world is an incomplete, not a maximal, state of affairs.[10] In the real world, if the statement "John lives in Paris" is true, it is also true that John lives in the capital of France and that he lives north of Milan and south of Stockholm. Such a set of requirements does not hold for the possible worlds of our beliefs—the so-called "doxastic" worlds. If it is true that John believes Tom lives in Paris, this does not mean that John believes Tom lives north of Milan, because John may suffer from a lack of geographic information.[11] Fictional worlds are as incomplete as doxastic worlds, but in a different way.

For example, at the beginning of Frederik Pohl and C. M. Kornbluth's novel *The Space Merchants,* we read: "I rubbed the depilatory soap over my face and rinsed it with the trickle from the fresh-water tap."[12] In a sentence referring to the real world, the mention of "fresh" water would seem redundant, since faucets are usually fresh-water faucets. But insofar as one suspects that this sentence is describing a fictional world, one understands that it is providing indirect information about a certain world where in normal sinks the fresh-water tap is opposed to the salt-water tap (while in our world the opposition is cold versus hot). Even if the story did not provide further information, readers would be eager to infer that it dealt with a science fiction world where there was a shortage of fresh water. In the absence of further information, we would be bound to think that both fresh water and salt water were normal H_2O. In this sense, it seems that fictional worlds are *parasitic* on the real world.[13] A fictional possible world is one in which everything is similar to our so-called real world, except for the variations explicitly introduced by the text.

Shakespeare, in *The Winter's Tale,* says that Scene 3 of Act 3 takes place in "Bohemia," a desert country near the sea. We know that Bohemia has no seacoast, just as there are no seaside resorts in Switzerland, but we take it for granted that—in the possible world of Shakespeare's play—"Bohemia" has a seacoast. By fictional agreement and a suspension of disbelief, we must take such variations as if they were true.[14]

It has been said that fictional characters are *underdetermined*—that is, we know only a few of their properties—while real individuals are *completely determined,* and we should be able to predicate of them each of their known attributes.[15] But although this is true from an ontological point of view, from an epistemological one it is exactly the opposite: nobody can assert all the properties of a given individual or of a given species, which are potentially infinite, while the properties of fictional characters are severely limited by the narrative text—and only those attributes mentioned by the text count for the identification of the character.

In fact, I know Leopold Bloom better than I know my own father. Who can say how many episodes of my father's life are unknown to me, how many thoughts my father never disclosed, how many times he concealed his sorrows, his quandaries, his weaknesses? Now that he is gone, I shall probably never discover those secret and perhaps fundamental aspects of his being. Like the historians described by Dumas, I muse and muse in vain about that dear ghost, lost to me forever. In contrast, I know everything about Leopold Bloom that I need to know—

and each time I reread *Ulysses* I discover something more about him.

Dealing with historical truths, historians can argue for centuries about whether a certain piece of information is relevant or not. For instance, is it relevant for the history of Napoleon to know what he ate just before the Battle of Waterloo? Most biographers would consider this detail irrelevant. Yet there might be scholars who strongly believe that food can have a decisive influence on human behavior. So this detail about Napoleon, if proved by some document, would be extremely important for their research.

In contrast, fictional texts tell us, rather precisely, which details are relevant for the interpretation of the story, the psychology of characters, and so on, and which ones are peripheral.

At the end of Book 2, Chapter 35, of *The Red and the Black,* Stendhal recounts how Julien Sorel tries to kill Madame de Rênal in the church of Verrières. Having said that Julien's arm is trembling, he concludes: "At that moment, the young priest who was officiating at the Mass rang the bell for the elevation of the Host. Madame de Rênal lowered her head, which for a moment became entirely hidden by the folds of her shawl. Julien could no longer see her features so distinctly. He fired a pistol shot at her, and missed. He fired a second shot; she fell."[16]

One page later, we are told that Madame de Rênal was not mortally wounded: the first bullet pierced her hat and the second struck her shoulder. It is interesting to note that, for reasons which have intrigued many critics,[17] Stendhal specifies where the second bullet ended up: it ricocheted off the shoulder bone and hit a Gothic pillar, breaking off an enormous chip of stone. But although he gives details about the trajectory of the second bullet, he says little about the first one.

People are still wondering what happened to Julien's first bullet. No doubt many of Stendhal's fans are trying to locate that church and find traces of the bullet (such as chips of stone missing from another column). In the same vein, many of James Joyce's fans have been known to gather in Dublin to find the pharmacy where Bloom bought lemon soap—and such a pharmacy exists, or still existed in 1965, when I bought the same kind of soap, probably produced by the apothecary just to please Joycean tourists.

Let's now suppose that a critic wants to interpret Stendhal's entire novel by taking that lost bullet as a starting point. There are crazier forms of criticism! Since the text does not make the lost bullet relevant (in fact, barely mentions it), we would be entitled to view such an interpretive strategy as farfetched. A fictional text tells us not only what is true and untrue in its narrative world, but also what is relevant and what can be disregarded as immaterial.

This is why we have the impression that we are in a position to make unquestionable assertions about fictional characters. It is absolutely true that Julien Sorel's first bullet missed its mark, just as it is absolutely true that Mickey Mouse is the boyfriend of Minnie.

Fictional versus Historical Assertions

Is a fictional assertion such as "Anna Karenina commits suicide by throwing herself in the path of a train" as true as the historical assertion "Adolf Hitler committed suicide, and his corpse was burned, in a bunker in Berlin"? Our instinctive response is that the statement about Anna refers to an invention, while the one about Hitler concerns something that really happened.

Thus, to be correct in terms of truth-conditional semantics, we should say that "It is true that Anna Karenina commits suicide by throwing herself in the path of a train" is merely another way of stating, "It is true in this world that the text of a Tolstoy novel asserts that Anna Karenina commits suicide by throwing herself in the path of a train."

If this is so, in logical terms the statement about Anna would be true *de dicto* and not *de re,* and from a semiotic point of view it would concern the *plane of expression* and not the *plane of content*—or, in Ferdinand de Saussure's terms, the level of the *signifier,* rather than that of the *signified.*

We can make true statements about fictional characters because what happens to them is recorded in a text, and a text is like a musical score. "Anna Karenina commits suicide by throwing herself in the path of a train" is true the same way it is true that Beethoven's Fifth Symphony is in C-minor (and not in F-major, like his Sixth) and begins with the musical phrase "G, G, G, E-flat."

Let me call this way of considering fictional assertions a "score-oriented approach." Yet such a position is not completely satisfying from the point of view of a reader's experience. Setting aside a lot of problems arising from the fact that reading a score is a complex process of interpretation, we can say that a musical score is a semiotic device which tells one how to produce a given sequence of sounds. Only after the transformation of a series of written signs into sounds can listeners say that they are enjoying Beethoven's Fifth Symphony. (This happens even to a very skilled musician who is able to read the score silently: in fact, he is reproducing the sounds in his mind.) When we say, "It is true in this world that the text of a Tolstoy novel asserts that Anna Karenina commits suicide by throwing herself in the path of a train," we are simply saying that it is true in this world that on a given printed page there is a sequence of written words which, when pronounced by the reader (even if only mentally), will enable the reader to realize that there is a narrative world where people like Anna and Vronsky exist.

But when speaking of Anna and Vronsky, we usually cease to think about the text in which we've read about their vicissitudes. We speak of them as if they were real people.

It is true (in this world) that the Bible opens with "Bereshit . . ."—"In the beginning . . ." But when we say that Cain killed his brother or that Abraham was on the verge of sacrificing his son—and often when we try to interpret these events morally or mystically—we do not refer to the original Hebrew score (which ninety percent of Bible readers are unfamiliar with); we speak about the *content,* not the *expression,* of the biblical text. It is true that we know Cain killed Abel because of the biblical written score, and it has been suggested that the existence of many nonphysical objects, called "social objects," ought to be or could be proved by a document. But we shall see below that (1) sometimes fictional characters existed before being recorded by a written document (as is the case with mythical and legendary figures), and (2) many fictional characters succeed in *surviving* the documents that recorded their existence.

As a matter of fact, nobody (I think) can reasonably deny that Adolf Hitler and Anna Karenina are two different kinds of entity, each having a different ontological status. I am not what in certain U.S. academic departments is derogatorily called a "textualist"—someone who believes (as some deconstructionists do) that there are no facts but only interpretations, that is, texts. Having developed a theory of interpretation based on the semiotics of C. S. Peirce, I assume that in order to implement any interpretation, there must be some fact to be interpreted.[18] Accepting, as I do, that there is a difference between facts which are certainly texts (like the physical copy of a book you are on the verge of reading) and facts which are not merely texts (like the fact that you are reading this book), I strongly believe that Hitler was a real human being (at least, I shall believe this until reliable historians produce contrary evidence, proving he was a robot built by Wernher von Braun), whereas Anna was merely imagined by a human mind and is, as some would say, an "artifact."[19]

Anyway, one could say that not only fictional assertions but also historical ones are *de dicto:* students who write that Hitler died in a bunker in Berlin are simply stating that this is true according to their history textbooks. In other words, except for judgments that depend on my direct experience (such as, "It's raining"), all the judgments I can make on the grounds of my cultural experience (that is, all those concerning the information recorded by an encyclopedia—that dinosaurs lived in the Jurassic Period, that Nero was mentally deranged, that the formula for sulfuric acid is H_2SO_4, and so on) are based on textual information. And even though they seem to express *de facto* truths, they are merely *de dicto.*

So let me use the term "encyclopedic truths" for all those items of common knowledge that I learn from an encyclopedia (such as the distance of the Sun from the Earth, or the fact that Hitler died in a bunker). I take these pieces of information to be true because I trust the scientific community, and I accept a sort of "division of cultural labor" by which I delegate specialized people to prove them. Yet encyclopedic assertions have limits. They are still subject to revision, since science is by definition always prepared to reconsider its own discoveries. If we keep an open mind, we must be ready to revise our opinions about Hitler's death whenever new documents are discovered, and to adjust our beliefs about the Sun's distance from the Earth as a result of new astronomical measurements. Moreover, the fact that Hitler died in a bunker has already been cast in doubt by some historians. It is conceivable that Hitler survived the fall of Berlin to the Allies and escaped to Argentina, that no body was burned in the bunker or that the burned body was of somebody else, that Hitler's suicide was invented for propaganda reasons by the Russians who arrived at the bunker, that the bunker never existed at all, since its exact location is still a matter of debate, and so on and so forth.

In contrast, the assertion "Anna Karenina committed suicide by throwing herself in the path of a train" cannot be cast in doubt.

Every assertion concerning encyclopedic truths can and frequently must be tested in terms of *external empirical legitimacy* (according to which one says, "Provide me with evidence that Hitler really died in the bunker"), while assertions about the suicide of Anna concern cases of *internal textual legitimacy* (meaning that one does not need to go outside the text to prove them). On the basis of such internal legitimacy, we would consider mad or ill-informed anyone who said that Anna Karenina married Pierre

Besuchov, while we would be less dismissive of a person who raised doubts about Hitler's death.

On the basis of the same internal legitimacy, the identity of fictional characters is unmistakable. In real life, we are still unsure of the identity of the Man in the Iron Mask; we do not know who Kaspar Hauser really was; we do not know whether Anastasia Nikolaevna Romanova was assassinated with the rest of the Russian royal family at Yekaterinburg, or survived and showed up as the charming claimant later played onscreen by Ingrid Bergman. In contrast, we read the stories of Arthur Conan Doyle being sure that, when Sherlock Holmes refers to Watson, he is always designating the same person and that the city of London does not have two such persons with the same name and the same profession —otherwise, the text would at least suggest that this is the case. I have elsewhere argued against Saul Kripke's theory of rigid designation,[20] but I willingly admit that such a notion is valid in fictional possible worlds. We can define Dr. Watson in many ways, but it is clear that he is the one who, in "A Study in Scarlet," is called Watson for the first time, by a character named Stamford, and that henceforth both Sherlock Holmes and Arthur Conan Doyle's readers, when using the name "Watson," intend to refer to that original baptism. It is possible that in a still-undiscovered novel, Conan Doyle says that Watson lied when claiming to have been wounded at the Battle of Maiwand or trained in medicine. But even in this case, Dr. Watson, unmasked as a fraud, will remain that person who, in "A Study in Scarlet," met Sherlock Holmes for the first time.

The problem of the strong identity of fictional characters is very important. Philippe Doumenc, in his book *Contre-enquête sur la mort d'Emma Bovary*,[21] tells the story of a police investigation proving that Madame Bovary did not poison herself but was murdered. Now, this novel acquires some flavor only because readers take it for granted that "in reality" Emma Bovary poisoned herself. Doumenc's novel can be enjoyed in the same way readers enjoy so-called "uchronic" stories, a temporal counterpart to utopias, a sort of HF ("history fiction," or science fiction about the past) in which, for example, an author might imagine what would have happened in Europe if Napoleon had won at Waterloo. A uchronic novel can be enjoyed only if the reader knows that Napoleon was defeated at Waterloo. Similarly, in order to enjoy Doumenc's novel, the reader must take it for granted that Madame Bovary really committed suicide. Otherwise, why write—or read—such a counter-story?

The Epistemological Function of Fictional Statements

We have not yet ascertained what kind of entities fictional characters are, outside the framework of a score-oriented approach. But we are in a position to say that fictional statements, because of the way we use them and think of them, are essential for clarifying our current notion of truth.

Suppose someone asked what it meant for an assertion to be true, and suppose we answered with the famous definition formulated by Alfred Tarski, according to which "Snow is white" is true if and only if snow is white. We would be saying something pretty interesting for stimulating intellectual discussion, but of little use to ordinary people (for instance, we would not know what kind of physical proof is sufficient to allow one to assert that snow is white). We should say, rather, that an assertion is unquestionably true when it is as irrefutable as the statement "Superman is Clark Kent."

In general, readers accept as irrefutable the idea that Anna Karenina committed suicide. But even if one wanted to look for external empirical proof, it suffices, for accepting the score-oriented approach (according to which it is true that Tolstoy, in a retrievable book, wrote thus-and-such), to have sense data confirming the assertion—whereas for the death of Hitler, every proof is further debatable.

In order to decide whether "Hitler died in the Berlin bunker" is unquestionably true, we must determine if we consider the statement to be as unquestionably true as "Superman is Clark Kent" or "Anna Karenina committed suicide by throwing herself in the path of a train." Only after performing this kind of test can we can say that "Hitler died in the Berlin bunker" is only probably true, perhaps highly probably true, but not beyond-the-shadow-of-a-doubt true (whereas "Superman is Clark Kent" can never be challenged). The pope and the Dalai Lama can spend years debating whether it is true that Jesus Christ is the Son of God, but (if they are well informed about literature and comic books) both must admit that Clark Kent is Superman, and vice versa. So this is the epistemological function of fictional statements: they can be used as a *litmus test* for the irrefutability of truths.

Fluctuating Individuals in Fluctuating Scores

To have suggested an alethic function for fictional truths still does not explain why we weep over the plight of fictional characters. Nobody is expected to be moved because *Tolstoy wrote that Anna Karenina died.* One is moved, at most, because *Anna Karenina died*—even if one is unaware of the fact that Tolstoy was the first to write about it.

Notice that what I have just said holds for Anna Karenina, Clark Kent, Hamlet, and many other figures, but not for every fictional character. Nobody (except specialists in Nero Wolfe trivia) would know who Dana Hammond was and what he did. One can at most say that in the novel entitled *In the Best Families* (published by Rex Stout in 1950), the text states that a certain banker named Dana Hammond did thus-and-such. Dana Hammond remains, so to speak, a prisoner of his original score. In contrast, if we wanted to quote a famous and infamous banker, we could mention the baron Nucingen, who somehow acquired the ability to live outside Balzac's books, where he was born. Nucingen became what certain aesthetic theories call a "universal type." Dana Hammond, alas, did not. Too bad for him.

In this sense, we must assume that certain fictional characters acquire a kind of existence independent of their original scores. How many people who know the fate of Anna Karenina have read Tolstoy's book? And how many of them have heard of her instead through movies (mainly two with Greta Garbo) and TV serials? I do not know the precise answer, but I can certainly say that many fictional characters "live" outside the score which has given them existence, and move to a zone of the universe which we find very difficult to delimit. Some of them even migrate from text to text, because the collective imagination has, over the course of centuries, made an emotional investment in them and transformed them into "fluctuating" individuals. Most came from great works of art or from myths, but certainly not all. Thus, our community of fluctuating entities includes Hamlet and Robin Hood, Heathcliff and Milady, Leopold Bloom and Superman.

Since I have always been fascinated by fluctuating characters, I once invented the following literary pastiche (I beg your pardon for this bit of self-plagiarism):

Vienna, 1950. Twenty years have gone by, but Sam Spade has not given up his search for the Maltese falcon. His contact now is Harry Lime, and they are talking furtively at the top of the Prater's Ferris wheel. They come down and walk over to the Mozart Café, where Sam is playing "As Time Goes By" on the lyre. At a table in the back, a cigarette hanging from the corner of his mouth, a bitter expression on his face, sits Rick. He has found a clue in the papers Ugarte has shown him, and now he shows Sam Spade a photograph of Ugarte: "Cairo!" murmurs the detective. Rick goes on with his account: when he triumphantly entered Paris with Captain Renault, as a member of De Gaulle's liberating army, he heard about a certain Dragon Lady (allegedly the assassin of Robert Jordan during the Spanish Civil War), whom the secret service had put on the trail of the falcon. She should be here any minute. The door opens and a woman appears. "Ilsa!" Rick cries. "Brigid!" Sam Spade cries. "Anna Schmidt!" Lime cries. "Miss Scarlett!" Sam cries, "you're back! Don't make my boss suffer any more."

Out of the darkness of the bar comes a man with a sarcastic smile on his face. It's Philip Marlowe. "Let's go, Miss Marple," he says to the woman. "Father Brown is waiting for us on Baker Street."[22]

One does not need to have read the original score in order to be acquainted with a fluctuating character. A lot of people know Ulysses without having read the *Odyssey*, and millions of kids who talk about Little Red Riding Hood have never read the two main sources of her story: the score by Charles Perrault and the one by the Brothers Grimm.

Becoming a fluctuating entity does not depend on the aesthetic qualities of the original score. Why do so many people grieve over the suicide of Anna Karenina, but only a small bunch of Victor Hugo addicts mourn the suicide of Cimourdain in *Ninety-Three*? Personally, I am more deeply touched at the fate of Cimourdain (a monumental hero) than at the fate of that poor lady. Too bad—the majority is against me. Who, except fans of French literature, remembers Augustin Meaulnes? Yet he was, and still is, the protagonist of a great novel by Alain Fournier: *Le Grand Meaulnes*. Certain sensitive readers can engage so deeply and passionately with these novels that they welcome Augustin Meaulnes and Cimourdain into their club. But most contemporary readers do not expect to come face-to-face with these characters on the street corner—whereas I recently read that, according to a survey, a fifth of British teenagers believe that Winston Churchill, Gandhi, and Dickens were fictional characters, while Sherlock Holmes and Eleanor Rigby were real.[23] So it seems that Churchill can acquire the privileged status of a fluctuating fictional entity, while Augustin Meaulnes cannot.

Certain characters are known more widely through their extratextual avatar than in the role they played in a specific score. Let's take the case of Little Red Riding Hood. In Perrault's text, the little girl is eaten by the wolf and the story stops there, inspiring serious reflections on the risks of imprudence. In the Grimms' text, the huntsman arrives, kills the wolf, and brings the child and her grandmother back to life. These days, the Little Red Riding Hood that all mothers and kids know is neither Perrault's nor the Grimms'. The happy ending comes from the Grimms' version, certainly, but many other details are a sort of merging of the two versions. The Little Red Riding Hood we know comes from a *fluctuating score,* more or less the one shared by all mothers and children's storytellers.

Many mythical characters belonged to this shared realm before they entered a specific text. Oedipus was a figure in many oral legends before becoming the subject of Sophocles' plays. After so many translations into movies, the Three Musketeers are no longer those of Dumas. Every reader of the Nero Wolfe stories knows that he lived in Manhattan, in a brownstone located somewhere on West 35th Street —but Rex Stout's novels mention at least ten different house numbers. At a particular moment, a sort of tacit agreement convinced Wolfe fans that the right number was 454; and on June 22, 1996, New York City and a club called the Wolfe Pack honored Rex Stout and Nero Wolfe with a bronze plaque at 454 West 35th Street, thus certifying this spot as the site of the fictional brownstone.

In the same way, Dido, Medea, Don Quixote, Madame Bovary, Holden Caulfield, Jay Gatsby, Philip Marlowe, Inspector Maigret, and Hercule Poirot all came to live outside their original scores

—and even people who have never read Vergil, Euripides, Cervantes, Flaubert, Salinger, Fitzgerald, Chandler, Simenon, or Christie can claim to make true statements about these characters. Being independent of the text and of the possible world in which they were born, such figures are (so to speak) circulating among us, and we have difficulty thinking of them as something other than real persons. Thus, we take them not only as models for our own life, but also as models for the lives of others. We might say that someone we know has an Oedipus complex, has a Gargantuan appetite, is as jealous as Othello, doubts like Hamlet, is a Scrooge.

Fictional Characters as Semiotic Objects

At this point, even though I have said that my concern here is not an ontological one, I cannot escape the basic ontological question: What sort of entity is a fictional character, and in what way does such a character—if not precisely exist—at least *subsist?*

A fictional character is certainly a *semiotic object.* By this I mean a set of properties that is recorded in the encyclopedia of a culture and that is conveyed by a given expression (a word, an image, or some other device). Such a cluster of properties is what we call the "meaning" or the "signified" of the expression.

Thus, the word "dog" conveys as its content the properties of being an animal, a mammal, a canid, a barking creature, man's best friend, and many other attributes mentioned in a comprehensive encyclopedia. These properties can, in turn, be *interpreted* by other expressions; and the series of these interrelated interpretations constitutes all of the notions concerning the term that are shared by a community and that are collectively recorded.

There are many kinds of semiotic objects, some of them representing classes of PhEO (for example, the class of "natural kinds," conveyed by words such as "horse," or of "artificial kinds," conveyed by words such as "table"), others representing abstract notions or ideal objects (such as "freedom" or "square root"), others that are of the class labeled "social objects" and that include marriages, money, university degrees—in general, any entity established by a collective agreement or law.[24] But there are also semiotic objects that represent individual persons or constructs and that are denoted by proper nouns such as "Boston" or "John Smith." I do not share the theory of "rigid designation," according to which a particular expression necessarily refers to the same thing in all possible worlds, regardless of any changes in circumstances. I believe strongly that every proper noun is a peg on which we hang a set of properties, so that the name "Napoleon" conveys specific properties: a man who was born in Ajaccio, served as a French general, became an emperor, won the Battle of Austerlitz, died on Saint Helena on May 5, 1821, and so on.[25]

The majority of semiotic objects share an important attribute: they have a possible referent. In other words, they have the property of being extant (as with the term "Mount Everest") or of having existed (as with "Cicero"), and frequently the term also conveys instructions for identifying the referent. Words like "horse" or "table" represent classes of PhEO; ideal objects like "freedom" or "square root" can be related to concrete individual cases (the Constitution of, say, the State of Vermont instantiates a case of freedom guaranteed to every citizen; 1.7320508075688772 is the square root of 3); and the same can be said of social objects (event X is a case of marriage). But there are cases of natural, artificial, abstract, or social kinds which cannot be related to any individual experience. Thus, we know the meaning (the alleged properties) of "unicorn," "Holy Grail," "the third law of robotics" as defined by Isaac Asimov, "square circle," and "Medea," but we are aware that we cannot isolate any instance of these objects in our physical world.

I would call such entities "purely intensional objects," if the term had not been used by Roman Ingarden for other purposes.[26] For Ingarden, purely intensional objects are artifacts such as a church or a flag—the former being more than the sum of its material parts, the latter being more than a piece of fabric, since it is endowed with a symbolic value based on social and cultural convention. In spite of this definition, the word "church" also conveys criteria for identifying a church, implying the materials it must be built of and its average size (a miniature replica of Reims Cathedral made of marzipan is not a church), and it is possible to find PhEOs which are churches (such Notre Dame in Paris, Saint Peter's in Rome, or Saint Basil's in Moscow). If, in contrast, we define fictional characters as purely intensional objects, we mean sets of properties that have no material equivalent in the real world. The expression "Anna Karenina" has no physical referent at all, and we cannot find in this world anything of which one could say, "This is Anna Karenina."

Let us, then, label fictional characters "*absolutely* intensional objects."

Carola Barbero has suggested that a fictional character is an "object of higher order"—that is, one of those objects that are something more than the sum of their properties. A higher-order object "is said to depend *generically* (and not *rigidly*) on its constitutive elements and relations, where 'generically' means that it needs *some* elements shaped in a specific form to be the object that it is, but it does *not* need *exactly* those specific elements."[27] What is crucial for the recognition of the object is that it maintains a Gestalt, a constant relation between its elements, even if these elements are no longer the same. For instance, "the 4:35 P.M. train from New York to Boston" is such an object, since it remains always recognizable as the same train even though its cars change every day. Not only that—it remains the same recognizable object even when its existence is denied, as in the case of the assertions "The 4:35 P.M. train from New York to Boston has been canceled" and "Because of technical difficulties, the 4:35 P.M. train from New York to Boston will depart at 5:00." A typical example of a higher-order object is a melody. Chopin's Piano Sonata No. 2 in B-Flat Minor, Opus 35, will remain melodically recognizable even when played on a mandolin. I concede that from an aesthetic point of view the result would be disastrous, but the melodic pattern would be preserved. And the piece would also be recognizable if some notes were dropped.

It would be interesting to determine which notes can be dropped without destroying the musical Gestalt and which ones are, on the contrary, essential —or "diagnostic"—for the melody to be identifiable. But this is not a theoretical problem; it is, rather, a task for a music critic, and it will have different solutions depending on the object being analyzed.

This point is important because the same problem exists when we analyze, instead of a melody, a fictional character. Would Madame Bovary still be Madame Bovary if she did not commit suicide? When reading the novel by Philippe Doumenc, we do indeed have the impression that we are dealing with the same character as the one in Flaubert's book. This "optical" illusion is due to the fact that Emma Bovary shows up at the beginning of the novel as already dead and is mentioned as the woman who *allegedly* committed suicide. The alternative proposed by the author (that she was murdered) remains the personal opinion of some of the characters in Doumenc's novel and does not alter Emma's main attributes.

Barbero quotes Woody Allen's story "The Kugelmass Episode," where Madame Bovary is brought by a sort of time machine to today's New York and has a love affair.[28] She seems a parody of Flaubert's Emma Bovary: she wears contemporary dresses and shops at Tiffany's. But she is still recognizable because she retains most of her diagnostic properties:

she is a member of the petite bourgeoisie, is married to a doctor, lives in Yonville, is dissatisfied with her small-town life, and is inclined to adultery. In Allen's story, Emma does not commit suicide, but—and this is essential for the ironic quality of the narrative— she is fascinating (and desirable) precisely because she is on the verge of committing suicide. Kugelmass must science-fictionally enter Flaubert's world *before* Emma has had her last adulterous relation, so that he does not arrive too late.

We can thus see that a fictional character remains the same even if he or she is set in a different context, provided that the *diagnostic* properties are retained. Which properties are really diagnostic must be defined for each character.[29]

Little Red Riding Hood is a girl, wears a red hood, and meets a wolf who later devours her and her grandmother. These are her diagnostic features, though different people can have different ideas about the age of the girl, the kind of food she has in her basket, and so on. This girl *fluctuates* in two ways: she lives outside her original score, and she is a sort of nebula whose borders are variable and imprecise. Yet some of her diagnostic properties remain invariable and make her recognizable in different contexts and situations. One could wonder what might have happened to Little Red Riding Hood if she had not encountered the wolf; but I have found, on various websites, many representations of a girl wearing a red hood and ranging in age from five to twelve, and I have always recognized the protagonist of the fairy tale. There was also an image that showed a sexy twenty-year-old blonde wearing a red cap, and I accepted her as a Little Red Riding Hood because the caption identified her as such; but I considered this a joke, a parody, a provocation. In order to be Little Red Riding Hood, a girl must exhibit at least *two* diagnostic properties: she must wear a red hood, and she must also be a *little* girl.

The very existence of fictional characters obliges semiotics to revise some of its approaches, which risk looking overly simple. The classic semantic triangle usually appears as shown in Figure 1. The inclusion of the referent in this triangle results from the fact that we frequently use verbal expressions to indicate something physically existing in our world. I follow Peter Strawson in assuming that mentioning or referring is not something an expression does, but rather something that a person can use an expression to do. Mentioning or referring is a function of the *use* of an expression.[30]

It is doubtful that we are implementing an act of reference when we say that dogs are animals or that

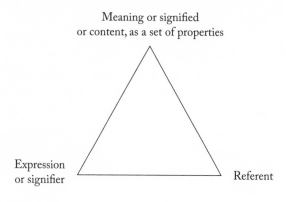

Meaning or signified
or content, as a set of properties

Expression
or signifier

Referent

FIGURE I

all cats are nice. It seems that in this case we are still making judgments about a given semiotic object (or class of objects), attributing it with specific properties.

A scientist might say that she has discovered a new property of apples, and she implements an act of reference when she states in her protocols that she tested those properties of apples on the real individual apples A, B, C (indicating the series of real objects she used to perform the experiments that legitimated her induction). But as soon as her discovery is accepted by the scientific community, that new property is attributed to apples in general and becomes a permanent part of the content of the word "apple."

We implement acts of reference when we speak of individuals—but there is a difference between referring to extant individuals and mentioning individuals who existed in the past. The content of the term "Napoleon" should include, among Napoleon's properties, the feature that he was dead on May 5, 1821. In contrast, the properties of the content of the term "Obama," when the term is used in 2010, must include the feature of being alive and president of the United States.[31]

The difference between referring to living individuals and mentioning individuals who lived in the past can be represented by two different semiotic triangles, as shown in Figures 2 and 3. In this case, speakers saying p when they refer to Obama invite their hearers to verify p (if they wish) in a precise spatio-temporal location of the physically existing world.[32] In contrast, whoever says p of Napoleon is not inviting people to verify p in a past world. Unless one has a time machine, one cannot go back into the past to check and see if Napoleon really won the Battle of Austerlitz. Every statement about Napoleon either asserts the properties conveyed by the word "Napoleon," or alludes to a newly discovered document that changes what we believed about him until now—for instance, that he died not on May 5 but on May 6. Only when the scientific community

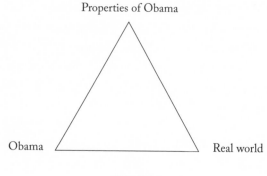

FIGURE 2

has verified that the document is a PhEO can we proceed to correct the public encyclopedia—that is, give the correct properties attributed to Napoleon as a semiotic object.

Napoleon could conceivably become the main character of a biographical reconstruction (or a historical novel) that tries to make him to live again in his time, reconstituting his actions and even his feelings. In this case, Napoleon would be very similar to a fictional character. We know that he really existed—but in order to observe and even participate in his life, we try to imagine his past world as if it were the possible world of a novel.

What actually happens in the case of fictional characters? It is true that some of them are introduced as people who lived "once upon a time" (like

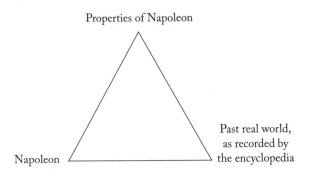

FIGURE 3

Little Red Riding Hood and Anna Karenina); but we have ascertained that by virtue of a narrative agreement, the reader is bound to take for true what is narrated and must pretend to live in the possible world of the narrative as if it were his or her real world. It is irrelevant whether the story is speaking about an allegedly living person (such as a specific detective currently working in Los Angeles) or whether it is speaking about an allegedly dead person. It is as if somebody were to tell us that *in this world* one of our relatives has just died: we would be emotionally engaged with a person who is still present in the world of our experience.

The semantic triangle might assume the form shown in Figure 4. Now we can better understand how one can get emotionally involved with the in-

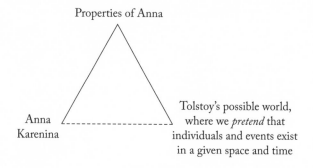

Properties of Anna

Anna
Karenina

Tolstoy's possible world,
where we *pretend* that
individuals and events exist
in a given space and time

FIGURE 4

habitants of a fictional possible world as if they were
real people. It happens only partly for the same reason we can be moved by a daydream in which a loved
one dies. In this latter case, at the end of our reverie
we come back to our everyday life and realize that
we had no cause for worry. But what would happen
if one lived in an uninterrupted daydream?

To be permanently emotionally involved with the
inhabitants of a fictional possible world, we must
satisfy two requirements: (1) we must live in the fictional possible world as if in an uninterrupted daydream, and (2) we must behave as if we were one of
the characters.

We have assumed that fictional characters are
born within the possible world of the narrative, and

that if and when they become fluctuating entities, they appear in other narratives or belong to a fluctuating score. We have also assumed that, according to a tacit agreement routinely made by readers of novels, we pretend to take the fictional possible world seriously. Thus, it can happen that, when we enter a very absorbing and captivating narrative world, a textual strategy can provoke something similar to a mystical *raptus* or a hallucination, and we simply *forget* we have entered a world that is merely possible.

This happens especially when we meet a character in its original score or in a new and enticing context; but since these characters are fluctuating and, so to speak, come and go in our mind (like the women in J. Alfred Prufrock's world, talking of Michelangelo), they are always ready to mesmerize us and make us believe that they are among us.

As for the second requirement, once we begin living in a possible world as if it were our real one, we can be disconcerted by the fact that in the possible world we are not, so to speak, formally registered. The possible world has nothing to do with us; we move within it as if we were the lost bullet of Julien Sorel, but our emotional involvement leads us to assume the personality of somebody else—a person who has the right to live there. Thus, we identify with one of the fictional characters.

When we awaken from a daydream in which a loved one dies, we realize that what we imagined was false, and we take as true the assertion, "My loved one is alive and well." In contrast, when the fictional hallucination ends—when we cease pretending that we are the fictional character, because, as Paul Valéry wrote, "le vent se lève, il faut tenter de vivre" ("the wind is rising, we must try to live")—we continue to take it as true that Anna Karenina committed suicide, that Oedipus killed his father, and that Sherlock Holmes lives on Baker Street.

I admit this is very peculiar behavior, but it happens often. After shedding tears, we close Tolstoy's book and return to the here-and-now. But we still assume that Anna Karenina committed suicide, and we think that whoever says she married Heathcliff is mad.

Being fluctuating entities, these faithful life-companions of ours (unlike other semiotic objects, which are culturally subject to revision)[33] will never change and will remain the agents of their actions forever. And because of the unalterability of their deeds, we can always claim it is true that they possessed certain qualities and behaved in a certain way.

Clark Kent is Superman now and till the end of time.

Other Semiotic Objects

Is there anyone else who shares the same fate? Yes: the heroes and gods of every mythology; legendary beings such as unicorns, elves, fairies, and Santa Claus; and nearly all of the entities revered by the world's various religions. It is obvious that for an atheist *every* religious entity is fictional, while for a believer there is a spiritual world of "supernatural objects" (gods, angels, and so on) inaccessible to our senses but absolutely "real"—and in this sense, an atheist and a believer rely on two different ontologies. But if Roman Catholics believe that a personal God truly exists and assume that the Holy Ghost proceeds from Him and His Son, then they must view Allah, Shiva, and the Great Spirit of the Prairies as mere fictions, invented by sacred narratives. Likewise, for a Buddhist the God of the Bible is a fictional individual, and the Algonquians' Gitchi Manitou is a fictional being for a Muslim or a Christian. This means that for a believer in a particular faith, all the religious entities of other religions—in other words, the overwhelming majority of such entities—are fictional individuals. So that we are bound to view approximately ninety percent of all religious entities as fictions.

The terms that designate religious entities have dual semantic reference. For a skeptic, Jesus Christ was a PhEO who existed for thirty-three years at the beginning of the first millennium; for a devout Christian, he is also an object that continues to subsist (in Heaven, according to the popular imagination) in a nonmaterial mode of existence.[34] There are many cases of dual semantic reference. But when it comes to ascertaining the true beliefs of ordinary people, some Britons (as we have noted) believe that Sherlock Holmes was a real person. Likewise, many Christian poets have been known to begin their verses by invoking the Muses or Apollo—and we cannot really tell if they are simply using a literary topos or are in some way taking seriously the divinities of Mount Olympus. Many mythological characters have become the protagonists of written narratives, and in a symmetrical way many protagonists of secular narratives have become very similar to the characters of mythological tales. The boundaries between legendary heroes, mythical gods, literary characters, and religious entities are often quite imprecise.

The Ethical Power of Fictional Characters

We have said that unlike all other semiotic objects, which are culturally subject to revision and perhaps similar only to mathematical entities, fictional characters will never change and will forever remain the agents of what they did. This is why they are important to us, especially from a moral point of view.

Imagine that we are watching a performance of Sophocles' *Oedipus Rex*. We desperately want Oedipus to take any other road instead of the one on which he met and murdered his father. We wonder why he wound up in Thebes and not, let us say, in Athens, where he could have married Phryne or Aspasia. Similarly, we read *Hamlet* wondering why such a nice boy couldn't marry Ophelia and live happily with her, after killing his scoundrel of an uncle and gently kicking his mother out of Denmark. Why couldn't Heathcliff show a little more fortitude in the face of his humiliations, waiting until he could marry Catherine and live with her as a worthy country gentleman? Why couldn't Prince Andrei recover from his mortal illness and marry Natasha? Why does Raskolnikov have the morbid idea of killing an old lady, instead of finishing his studies and becoming a respected professional? Why, when Gregor

Samsa is transformed into a pathetic bug, doesn't a beautiful princess arrive on the scene, kiss him, and transform him into the most handsome young man in Prague? Why, in the arid hills of Spain, couldn't Robert Jordan beat those fascist pigs and rejoin his sweet Maria?

In principle, we can make all of these things happen. All we have to do is rewrite *Oedipus, Hamlet, Wuthering Heights, War and Peace, Crime and Punishment, The Metamorphosis,* and *For Whom the Bell Tolls.* But do we really want to?

The devastating experience of finding that, in spite of our wishes, Hamlet, Robert Jordan, and Prince Andrei die — that things happen in a certain way, and forever, no matter what we yearn for or hope for in the course of our reading — makes us shiver as we feel the finger of Destiny. We realize that we cannot know whether Ahab will capture the White Whale. The real lesson of *Moby-Dick* is that the Whale goes wherever She wants. The compelling nature of the great tragedies stems from the fact that their heroes, instead of escaping an atrocious fate, plunge into the abyss — which they have dug with their own hands — because they have no idea what awaits them; and we, who clearly see where they are headed so blindly, cannot stop them. We have cognitive access to the world of Oedipus, and we know everything about him and Jocasta—but they, even though they live in a world that depends parasitically on our own, do not know anything about us. Fictional characters cannot communicate with people in the real world.[35]

Such a problem is not as whimsical as it seems. Please try to take it seriously. Oedipus cannot conceive of the world of Sophocles—otherwise, he would not wind up marrying his mother. Fictional characters live in an incomplete—or, to be ruder and politically incorrect—*handicapped* world.

But when we truly understand their fate, we begin to suspect that we too, as citizens of the here-and-now, frequently encounter our destiny simply because we think of our world in the same way that fictional characters think of theirs. Fiction suggests that perhaps our view of the actual world is as imperfect as the view that fictional characters have of their world. This is why successful fictional characters become supreme examples of the "real" human condition.

4

My Lists

I had a Catholic education, and thus became used to reciting and listening to litanies. Litanies are by nature repetitious. Usually they are lists of laudatory phrases, as with the Litanies of the Virgin: "Sancta Maria," "Sancta dei genitrix," "Sancta Virgo virginum," "Mater Christi," "Mater divinae gratiae," "Mater purissima," and so on.

Litanies, like phone books and catalogues, are a type of list. They are cases of *enumeration*. Perhaps, at the beginning of my career as a narrator of fiction, I did not realize how fond I was of lists. Now, after five novels and some other literary attempts, I am in a position to draw up a complete list of my lists. But such a venture would take too much time, so I'll limit myself to quoting some of my enumerations, and—as proof of my humility—comparing them with some of the greatest catalogues in the history of world literature.

Practical and Poetic Lists

First of all, we must distinguish between lists that are "practical" (or "pragmatic") and those that are "literary" or "poetic" or "aesthetic"—the last of these adjectives being more comprehensive than the prior two, since there are not only verbal lists, but also visual, musical, and gestural ones.[1]

A practical list might be a shopping list, a library catalogue, the inventory of objects in any place (such as an office, archive, or museum), a restaurant menu, or even a dictionary, which records all the words in the lexicon of a given language. Such lists have a purely referential function, since their items designate corresponding objects; and if these objects didn't exist, the list would simply be a false document. Recording, as they do, things that exist—that are physically present somewhere—practical lists are *finite*. For this reason, they may not be altered, in the sense that it would be pointless to include in a museum catalogue a painting that is not held in the museum's collection.

In contrast, poetic lists are *open*, and in some way presuppose a final *etcetera*. They aim at suggesting an infinity of persons, objects, events, for two reasons: (1) the writer is aware that the quantity of things is too vast to be recorded; (2) the writer takes pleasure

—sometimes a purely auditory pleasure—in cease-less enumeration.[2]

In their own way, practical lists represent a form, because they confer unity on a set of objects that, no matter how dissimilar, are subject to a *contextual pressure*—meaning that they are related simply because they are all in the same place, or because they constitute the goal of a certain project (an example would be the guest list for a party). A practical list is never incongruous, provided we can identify the criterion of assembly that governs it. In Thornton Wilder's novel *The Bridge of San Luis Rey,* a group of people have nothing in common except the *accidental fact* that they are crossing the bridge at the precise moment of its collapse.

A fine model of the practical list is the famous enumeration by Leporello in Mozart's *Don Giovanni.* Don Giovanni has seduced a great number of countrywomen, maids, ladies of the town, countesses, baronesses, marchionesses, princesses—women of all ranks, shapes, and ages. But Leporello is a precise bookkeeper, and his catalogue is mathematically complete:

> In Italy six hundred and forty,
> In Germany two hundred and thirty-one,
> One hundred in France, ninety-one in Turkey,
> But in Spain there are already one thousand and three.

That makes 2,065 in all, no more, no less. If Don Giovanni were to seduce Donna Anna or Zerlina the next day, then there would be a new list.

It is obvious why people make practical lists. But why do they make poetic ones?

The Rhetoric of Enumeration

As I have said, writers make lists either when the set of items they are dealing with is so vast that it eludes their ability to master it, or when they become enamored of the sound of the words that name a series of things. In the latter case, one moves from a list concerned with *referents* and *signifieds* to a list concerned with *signifiers*.

Think of the genealogy of Jesus at the beginning of the Gospel according to Matthew. We are free to doubt the historical existence of many of those ancestors, but certainly Matthew (or someone in his stead) wanted to introduce "real" persons into the world of his beliefs, so the list had a practical value and a referential function. In contrast, the Litanies of the Blessed Virgin—a catalogue of attributes borrowed either from passages of Scripture or from tradition and popular devotion—must be recited like a mantra, much like the Buddhists' "Om mani padme hum." It doesn't matter so much whether the *virgo* is *potens* or *clemens* (in any case, until the Second Vatican Council, litanies were recited in Latin by the faithful, the majority of whom did not understand that tongue). What matters is that one is seized by the hypnotic sound of the list. Just as with the Litanies of the Saints, what matters is not which names are present or absent, but the fact that they are rhythmically enunciated for a sufficiently long period of time.

It was the latter kind of motivation that was largely analyzed and defined by ancient rhetoricians, who examined many cases in which it was less important to hint at inexhaustible quantities than to attribute properties to things in an aggregative way, often from pure love of iteration.

The various forms of lists would generally consist of *accumulations*—that is, sequences and juxtaposition of linguistic terms belonging to the same conceptual sphere. One form of such accumulation was known as *enumeratio*, which regularly appears in medieval literature. Sometimes the terms of the list seem to lack consistency and homogeneity, because the aim was to define the properties of God—and God, according to Pseudo-Dionysius the Areopagite, can be described only by means of dissimilar images. Hence, in the fifth century, Ennodius wrote that Christ was the "source, way, right, rock, lion, light-bearer, lamb; door, hope, virtue, word, wisdom, prophet; victim, scion, shepherd, mountain, snare, dove; flame, giant, eagle, spouse, patience, worm."[3] Such lists, as well as the Litanies of the Virgin, are termed *panegyric* or *encomiastic*.

Another form of accumulation is the *congeries* —a sequence of words or phrases that all mean the same thing, and in which the same thought is reproduced in myriad ways. This corresponds to the principle of "oratorical amplification," which is famously illustrated by Cicero's first oration against Catiline in the Roman Senate (63 B.C.): "When, O Catiline, do you mean to cease abusing our patience? How long is that madness of yours still to mock us? When is there to be an end of that unbridled audacity of yours, swaggering about as it does now? Do not the nightly guards placed on the Palatine Hill—do not the watches posted throughout the city—does not the alarm of the people, and the union of all good men—does not the precaution taken of assembling the senate in this most defensible place—do not the looks and countenances of this venerable body here present, have any effect upon you? Do you not feel that your plans are detected? Do you not see that your conspiracy is already arrested and rendered powerless by the knowledge which every one here possesses of it?"[4] And so on.

Slightly different forms are the *incrementum*, also known as the *climax* or *gradatio*. Even though they still refer to the same conceptual field, at every step they say something more, or with greater intensity. An example of this can be found, again, in Cicero's first oration against Catiline: "You do nothing, you plan nothing, you think of nothing which I not only do not hear, but which I do not see and know every particular of."[5]

Classical rhetoric also defines enumeration by *anaphora* and enumeration by *asyndeton* or *polysyndeton*. Anaphora is the repetition of the same word at the beginning of every phrase or of every line of verse. This may not always constitute what we would call a list. There is a beautiful example of anaphora in the poem "Possibilities," by Wisława Szymborska.

> I prefer movies.
> I prefer cats.
> I prefer the oaks along the Warta.
> I prefer Dickens to Dostoyevsky.
> I prefer myself liking people to myself loving mankind.

I prefer keeping a needle and thread on hand, just in case.

I prefer the color green.

And so on, for other twenty-six lines.[6]

Asyndeton is a rhetorical strategy that eliminates conjunctions between elements in a series. A good example is the classic opening of Ariosto's *Orlando Furioso:* "Le dame, i cavalier, l'arme, gli amori / le cortesie, le audaci imprese io canto."[7]

The opposite of asyndeton is polysyndeton, which links *all* elements with conjunctions. In Book 2 of Milton's *Paradise Lost,* line 949 illustrates asyndeton, followed in the next line by polysyndeton:

With head, hands, wings, or feet pursues his way
And swims or sinks, or wades, or creeps, or flyes.

But in traditional rhetoric, there is no specific definition of what strikes us as the dizzying voracity of the list—especially long lists of assorted things, as in this short passage from Italo Calvino's novel *The Nonexistent Knight:*

You must sympathize: we are country girls. . . . Apart from religious services, tridua, novenas, work in the fields, threshing, the vintage, the whipping of servants, incest, fires, hangings, invading armies, sack, rape, and pestilence, we have seen nothing.[8]

When I was writing my doctoral dissertation on medieval aesthetics, I read lots of medieval poetry and discovered how greatly the Middle Ages loved enumeration. Take, for instance, this praise of the city of Narbonne by Sidonius Apollinaris, who lived in the fifth century A.D.:

> Salve Narbo, potens salubritate, urbe et rure simul bonus videri, muris, civibus, ambito, tabernis, portis, porticibus, foro theatro, delubris, capitoliis, monetis, thermis, arcubus, horreis, macellis, pratis, fontibus, insulis, salinis, stagnis, flumine, merce, ponte, ponto; unus qui venerere iure divos Laeneum, Cererem, Palem, Minervam spicis, palmite, pascuis, trapetis.

You needn't know any Latin in order to appreciate such lists. What counts is the obstinacy of the enumeration; the topic of the list—in this case, the architectural elements of the city—is irrelevant. The only true purpose of a good list is to convey the idea of infinity and the vertigo of the *etcetera*.

As I grew in age and wisdom, I discovered the lists of Rabelais and of Joyce. Lists represent an immense part of the vast opus of each of these authors. But since I cannot avoid these models, which played a decisive role in my development as a writer, let me quote at least two passages.

The first comes from *Gargantua:*

There he played at flush, at love, at primero, at the chess, at the beast, at Reynard the fox, at the rifle, at the squares, at trump, at the cows, at the prick and spare not, at the lottery, at the hundred, at the chance or mumchance, at the peeny, at three dice or maniest bleaks, at the unfortunate woman, at the tables, at the fib, at nivinivinack, at the pass ten, at the lurch, at one-and-thirty, at doublets or queen's game, at post and pair, or even at the faily sequence, at the French tric-trac, at three hundred, at the long tables or ferkeering, at the unlucky man, at feldown, at the last couple in hell, at tod's body, at the hock, at needs must, at the surly, at the dames or draughts, at the lansquenet, at bob and mow, at the cuckoo, at primus secundus, at puff, or let him speak that hath it, at mark-knife, at the keys, at take nothing and throw out, at span-counter, at the marriage, at even or odd, at the frolic or jackdaw, at cross or pile, at the opinion, at ball and huckle-bones, at who doth the one, doth the other, at ivory balls, at the billiards, at the sequences, at bob and hit, at the ivory bundles, at the owl, at the tarots, at the charm-ing of the hare, at losing load him, at pull yet a little, at he's gulled and esto, at trudgepig, at the torture, at the magatapies, at the handruff, at the horn, at the click, at the flowered or Shrovetide ox, at honours, at the madge-owlet, at pinch without laughing, at tilt at weeky, at prickle me tickle me, at ninepins, at the un-shoeing of the ass, at the cock quintin, at the cocksess, at tip and hurl, at hari hohi, at the flat bowls, at I set me down, at the veer and turn, at earl beardy, at rogue and ruffian, at the old mode, at bumbatch touch, at draw the spit, at the mysterious trough, at put out, at the short bowls, at gossip lend me your sack, at the dapple-grey, at the ramcod ball, at cock and crank it, at thrust out the harlot, at break-pot, at Marseilles figs, at my desire, at nicknamry, at twirly whirlytrill, at stick and hole, at the rush bundles, at boke or him or flaying the fox ...[9]

And so on, for several more pages.

The second excerpt comes from Joyce's *Ulysses* and represents a small portion of the seventeenth chapter (which is more than a hundred pages). It lists only some of the items Bloom can find in his kitchen sideboard:

What did the first drawer unlocked contain? A Vere Foster's handwriting copybook, property of Milly (Millicent) Bloom, certain pages of which bore diagram drawings, marked *Papli*, which showed a large globular head with 5 hairs erect, 2 eyes in profile, the trunk full front with 3 large buttons, 1 triangular foot: 2 fading photographs of queen Alexandra of England and of Maud Branscombe, actress and professional beauty: a Yuletide card, bearing on it a pictorial representation of a parasitic plant, the legend *Mizpah,* the date Xmas 1892, the name of the senders: from Mr + Mrs M. Comerford, the versicle: *May this Yuletide bring to thee, Joy and peace and welcome glee:* a butt of red partly liquefied sealing wax, obtained from the stores department of Messrs Hely's, Ltd., 89, 90, and 91 Dame street: a box containing the remainder of a gross of gilt "J" pennibs, obtained from same department of same firm: an old sandglass which rolled containing sand which rolled: a sealed prophecy (never unsealed) written by Leopold Bloom in 1886 concerning the consequences of the passing into law of William Ewart Gladstone's Home Rule bill of 1886 (never passed into law): a bazaar ticket, no. 2004, of S. Kevin's Charity Fair, price 6d, 100 prizes: an infantile epistle, dated, small em monday, reading: capital pee Papli comma capital aitch How are you note of interrogation capital eye I am very well full stop new paragraph signature with flourishes capital em Milly no stop: a cameo brooch, property of Ellen Bloom (born Higgins), deceased: a cameo scarfpin, property of Rudolph Bloom (born Virag), deceased: 3 typewritten letters, addressee, Henry Flower, c/o. P.O. Westland Row, addresser, Martha Clifford, c/o. P.O. Dolphin's Barn: the transliterated name and address of the addresser of the 3 letters in reversed alphabetic boustrophedonic punctated quadrilinear cryptogram (vowels suppressed) N. IGS./WI. UU. OX/W. OKS. MH/Y. IM: a press cutting from an English weekly periodical *Modern Society,* subject corporal chastisement in girls' schools: a pink ribbon which had festooned an Easter egg in the year 1899: two partly uncoiled rubber preservatives with reserve pockets, purchased by post from Box 32, P. O., Charing Cross, London, W.C.: 1 pack of 1 dozen creamlaid envelopes and feintruled notepaper, watermarked, now reduced by 3: some assorted Austrian-Hungarian coins: 2 coupons of the Royal and Privileged Hungarian Lottery: a lowpower magnifying glass . . .[10]

Under such influences, and with a Rabelaisian taste for accumulation, in the early 1960s I wrote a letter to my son (at that time one year old) telling him that as soon as possible I wanted to give him a great many toy weapons, in order to make him a staunch pacifist when he grew up. Here is the arsenal I mentioned:

So your presents will be guns. Double-barreled shotguns. Repeaters. Submachine guns. Cannons. Bazookas. Sabers. Armies of lead soldiers in full battle dress. Castles with drawbridges. Fortresses to besiege. Casemates, powder magazines, destroyers, jets. Machine guns, daggers, revolvers. Colts and Winchesters. Chassepots, 91's, Garands, shells, arquebuses, culverins, slingshots, crossbows, lead balls, catapults, firebrands, grenades, ballistas, swords, pikes, battering rams, halberds, and grappling hooks. And pieces of eight, just like Captain Flint's (in memory of Long John Silver and Ben Gunn), and dirks, the kind that Don Barrejo liked so much, and Toledo blades to knock aside three pistols at once and fell the Marquis of Montelimar, or using the Neapolitan feint with which the Baron de Sigognac slayed the evil ruffian who tried to steal his Isabelle. And there will be battle-axes, partisans, misericords, krises, javelins, scimitars, darts, and sword-sticks like the one John Carradine held when he was electrocuted on the third rail—and if nobody remembers that, it's their tough luck. And pirate cutlasses to make Carmaux and Van Stiller blanch, and damascened pistols like none Sir James Brook ever saw (otherwise he wouldn't have given up in the face of the sardonic, umpteenth cigarette of the Portuguese); and stilettos with triangular blades, like the one with which Sir William's disciple, as the day was gently dying at Clignancourt, killed the assassin Zampa, who killed his own mother, the old and sordid Fipart; and poires d'angoisse, like those inserted into the mouth of the jailer La Ramée while the Duke of Beaufort, the hairs of his coppery beard made even more fascinating thanks to the constant attention of a leaden comb, rode off, anticipating with joy the wrath of Mazarin; and muzzles loaded with nails, to be fired by men whose teeth are red with betel stains; and guns with mother-of-pearl stocks, to be grasped on Arab chargers with glistening coats; and lightning-fast bows, to turn the sheriff of Nottingham green with envy; and scalping knives, such as Minnehaha might have had, or (since you are bilingual) Winnetou. A small, flat pistol to tuck into a waistcoat under a frock coat, for the feats of a gentleman thief, or a ponderous Luger weighing down a pocket or filling an armpit à la Michael Shayne. And shotguns worthy of Jesse James and Wild Bill Hickok, or Sambigliong, muzzle-loading. In other words, weapons. Many weapons. These, my boy, will be the highlight of all your Christmases.[11]

When starting to write *The Name of the Rose*, I borrowed from ancient chronicles the names of various kinds of vagabonds, burglars, and wandering heretics, to give a sense of the great social and religious confusion that prevailed during the fourteenth century in Italy. My list was justified by the quantity of such irregular and erratic people, but it is clear that I indulged in expanding that hodgepodge out of a fondness for the *flatus vocis*—the pure pleasure of the sound.

In broken words, obliging me to recall what little I knew of Provençal and of Italian dialects, he told me the story of his flight from his native village and his roaming about the world. And in his story I recognized many men I had already known or encountered along the road, and I now recognize many more that I have met since. . . .

. . . Salvatore journeyed through various lands, from his native Montferrat toward Liguria, then up through Provence into the lands of the King of France. Salvatore wandered through the world, begging, pilfering, pretending to be ill, entering the temporary service of some lord, then again taking to the forest or the high road. From the story he told me, I pictured him among those bands of vagrants that in the years that followed I saw more and more often roaming about Europe: false monks, charlatans, swindlers, cheats, tramps and tatterdemalions, lepers and cripples, jugglers, invalid mercenaries, wandering Jews escaped from the infidels with their spirit broken, lunatics, fugitives under banishment, malefactors with an ear cut off, sodomites, and along with them ambulant artisans, weavers, tinkers, chair-menders, knife-grinders, basket-weavers, masons, and also rogues of every stripe, forgers, scoundrels, cardsharps, rascals, bullies, reprobates, recreants, frauds, hooligans, simoniacal and embezzling canons and priests, people who lived on the credulity of others, counterfeiters of bulls and papal seals, peddlers of indulgences, false paralytics who lay at church doors, vagrants fleeing from convents, relic-sellers, pardoners, soothsayers and fortunetellers, necromancers, healers, bogus alms-seekers, fornicators of every sort, corruptors of nuns and maidens by deception and violence, simulators of dropsy, epilepsy, hemorrhoids, gout, and sores, as well as melancholy madness. There were those who put plasters on their bodies to imitate incurable ulcerations, others who filled their mouths with a blood-colored substance to feign accesses of consumption, rascals who pretended to be weak in one of their limbs, carrying unnecessary crutches and imitating the falling sickness, scabies, buboes, swellings, while applying bandages, tincture of saffron, carrying irons on their hands, their heads swathed, slipping into the churches stinking, and suddenly fainting in the squares, spitting saliva and popping their eyes, making the nostrils spurt blood concocted of blackberry juice and vermilion, to wrest food or money from the frightened people who recalled the church fathers' exhortations to give alms: Share your bread with the hungry, take the homeless to your hearth, we visit Christ, we house Christ, we clothe Christ, because as water purges fire, so charity purges our sins.

Long after the events I am narrating, along the course of the Danube I saw many, and still see some, of these charlatans who had their names and their subdivisions in legions, like the devils. It was like a mire that flowed over the paths of our world, and with them mingled preachers in good faith, heretics in search of new victims, agitators of discord. . . .

. . . And he joined penitential sects and groups whose names he could not pronounce properly and whose doctrine he defined in highly unlikely terms. I deduced that he had encountered Patarines and Waldensians, and perhaps Catharists, Arnoldists, and Umiliati, and that, roaming about the world, he had passed from one group to another, gradually assuming as a mission his vagrant state, and doing for the Lord what he had done till then for his belly.[12]

Form and List

Only later did I begin to ponder a possible semiotics of lists, when writing about the "accumulations" of the French artist Arman: assemblages—tangible lists—of various types of eyeglasses or wristwatches squeezed into a plastic container. At that time, I reflected on the fact that the first occurrence of the list as a literary device is in Homer: the so-called catalogue of ships in Book 2 of the *Iliad*.[13] As a matter of fact, Homer offers us a beautiful opposition between the representation of a complete and finite form and that of an incomplete and potentially infinite list.

A complete and finite form is the shield of Achilles in Book 18 of the *Iliad*. Hephaestus divides this immense shield into five zones, and depicts two populous cities. In the first, he portrays a wedding feast, and a crowded forum where a trial is being held. The second scene shows a besieged castle; on the ramparts, wives, maidens, and old men watch the action. Led by Minerva, the enemy forces advance and, as the people lead their livestock to a river, prepare an ambush. A great battle ensues. Then Hephaestus sculpts a fertile, well-ploughed field of grain crisscrossed by ploughmen and their oxen; a vineyard full of ripe grapes, golden shoots, and vines trained on silver poles, surrounded by a wrought-iron fence; a herd of cattle made of gold and tin racing to the pasture along the banks of a river, whose waters flow through the reeds. Suddenly, two lions appear and pounce on the heifers and the bull, wounding it and dragging it along as it bellows pitifully. By the time the herdsmen approach with their dogs, the wild beasts are devouring the disemboweled bull, and the mastiffs just bark at them powerlessly. Hephaestus's final panel depicts flocks of sheep in a bucolic valley landscape dotted with huts and paddocks and dancing youths and virgins. The latter are clad in diaphanous robes and crowned with garlands; the former are wearing doublets, with golden daggers at their sides; and all are whirling round and round like a potter's wheel. Many people watch the dancing, after which come three tumblers who sing as they perform their acrobatics. The mighty river Oceanus surrounds every scene and separates the shield from the rest of the universe.

My summary is incomplete: the shield has so many scenes that, unless we imagine Hephaestus using microscopically small goldsmithery, it is difficult to envision the object in all its wealth of detail. What's more, the portrayal occupies not only space but time: the various events follow one another, as if the shield were a cinema screen or a long cartoon strip. The perfect circular nature of the artifact suggests that there is nothing else beyond its bounds: it is a *finite* form.

Homer was able to imagine the shield because he had a clear idea of the agricultural and military culture of his own day. He knew his world; he knew its laws, causes, and effects. This is why he was able to *give it a form.*

In Book 2, Homer wants to evoke a sense of the magnitude of the Greek army, and convey some idea of the mass of men the terrified Trojans see spreading out along the seashore. At first, he attempts a comparison with a flock of geese or cranes that seem to cross the sky like thunder, but no useful metaphor comes to his aid, and he (here in the classic translation by Samuel Butler) calls on the Muses for help:

> And now, O Muses, dwellers in the mansions of Olympus, tell me—for you are goddesses and are in all places so that you see all things, while we know nothing but by report—who were the chiefs and princes of the Danaans? As for the common soldiers, they were so that I could not name every single one of them though I had ten tongues, and though my voice failed not and my heart were of bronze within me, unless you, O Olympian Muses, daughters of aegis-bearing Jove, were to recount them to me. Nevertheless, I will tell the captains of the ships and all the fleet together.

This looks like a shortcut, but the shortcut takes him nearly three hundred lines of the Greek original, in order to take into account 1,186 ships. Apparently, the list is finite (there should not be other captains and other ships), but since he cannot say how many men are serving under each leader, the number he alludes to is still indefinite.

The Ineffable

With his catalogue of ships, Homer does not merely give us a splendid example of a list, but also presents what has been called the "topos of ineffability."[14] This topos occurs several times in Homer (for example, in the *Odyssey,* Book 4, lines 273ff, Butler's translation: "I cannot indeed name every single one of the exploits of Ulysses . . ."); and sometimes the poet—faced with an infinity of things or events to mention—decides to keep silent. Dante feels unable to name all the angels in Heaven, because he does not know their vast number (in Canto 29 of the *Paradiso,* it is said to exceed the capacity of the human mind). So the poet, faced with the ineffable, instead of trying to compile an incomplete series of names, prefers to express the ecstasy of ineffability. At most, to convey an idea of the incalculable number of angels, he alludes to the legend in which the inventor of chess asked the king of Persia, as a reward for his invention, to give him one grain of wheat for the first square on the board, two for the second, four for the third and so on until the sixty-fourth, thus reaching an astronomical number of grains: "In number did outmillion the account / Reduplicate upon the chequer'd board."[15]

In other cases, faced with something that is vast or unknown, which we still do not know enough about or which we shall never know enough about, the author proposes a list as a specimen, example, or indication, leaving the reader to imagine the rest.

In my novels, there is at least one point where I inserted a list simply because I was dazzled by the sense of the ineffable. I was not touring Heaven, like Dante, but in a more terrestrial way was visiting the coral reefs of the South Seas. It was when I was writing *The Island of the Day Before,* and I got the impression that no human tongue could describe the abundance, the variety, the incredible colors of the corals and fishes of that region. But even if I had been able to do that, my character Roberto, shipwrecked on those coasts in the seventeenth century and probably the first human being ever to visit that reef, could not have found words to express his ecstasy.

My problem was that South Sea corals display an infinity of shades (people who have seen only the poor corals of other seas can have no real idea of what this means), and I was obliged to represent colors by words, via the rhetorical device known as hypotyposis. The challenge was to evoke an enormous variety of colors through a great variety of words, never using the same color term twice and casting about for synonyms.

Here is part of my double list of corals (and fishes) and words:

For a while he saw only patches; then, like a seaman on a ship in a foggy night, approaching a cliff, which suddenly looms, sheer, before his eyes, he saw the rim of the chasm over which he was swimming. He took off the mask, emptied it, replaced it, holding it with his hand, and with a slow kicking motion he headed for the spectacle he had just glimpsed. So this was coral. His first impression, to judge by his later notes, was confused, dazed. It was an impression of being in the shop of a merchant of stuffs who draped before his eyes sendals and taffetas, brocades, satins, damasks, velvets, and bows, fringes and furbelows, and then stoles, pluvials, chasubles, dalmatics. But the stuffs moved with a life of their own, sensual as oriental dancing-maids. In that landscape—which Roberto does not describe because, seeing it for the first time, he cannot find in his memory images capable of translating it into words—now suddenly a host of creatures erupted and these, indeed, he recognized, or at least could compare to others previously seen. They were fish, intersecting like shooting stars in an August sky, but in composing and distributing the hues and patterns of their scales, Nature must have wanted to demonstrate the variety of accents that exists in the Universe and how many can be placed together on a single surface. Some were striped in several colors, lengthwise or breadthwise, some had slanting lines and others had curving lines. Some seemed worked like intarsia with crumbs of spots brilliantly deployed, some were speckled or dotted, others patched, spattered, or minutely stippled, or veined like marble. Still others had a serpentine design, or a pattern like several interwoven chains. Some were spotted with enamels, sown with shields and rosettes. And one, beautiful above the rest, seemed circled with cordons forming two rows of grapes and milk; and it was miraculous that not once did the row that enfolded the belly fail to continue on the flank, as if it were the work of an artist's hand. Only at that moment, seeing against the background of fish the coralline forms he had not been able to recognize at first, could Roberto make out bunches of bananas, baskets of bread rolls, corbeilles of bronze loquats over which canaries and geckos and hummingbirds were hovering. He was above a garden, no, he was mistaken, now it seemed a petrified forest, and at the next moment there were mounds, folds, shores, gaps and grottoes, a single slope of living stones on which a vegetation not of this earth was composed in squat forms, or round, or scaly, that seemed to wear a granulated coat of mail, or else gnarled, or else coiled. But, different as they were, they were all stupendous in their grace and loveliness, to such a degree that even those worked with feigned negligence, roughly shaped, displayed their roughness with majesty: they were monsters, true, but monsters of beauty. Or else (Roberto crosses out and revises, and is unable to report, like someone who must describe for the first time a squared circle, a coastal plain, a noisy silence, a nocturnal rainbow) what he was seeing were shrubs of cinnabar. Perhaps, holding his breath so long, he had grown befuddled, and the water entering his mask blurred shapes and hues. He thrust his head up to let air into his lungs, and resumed floating along the edge of the barrier, following its rifts and anfracts, past corridors of chalk in which vinous harlequins were stuck, while on a promontory he saw reposing, stirred by slow respiration and a waving of claws, a lobster crested with whey over a coral net (this coral looked like the coral he knew, but was spread out like the legendary cheese of Fra Stefano, which never ends). What he saw now was not a fish, nor was it a leaf; certainly it was a living thing, like two broad slices of whitish matter edged in crimson and with a feather fan; and where you would have expected eyes, there were two horns of whipped sealing-wax. Cypress-polyps, which in their vermicular writhing revealed the rosy color of a great central lip, stroked plantations of albino phalli with amaranth glandes; pink minnows dotted with olive grazed on ashen cauliflowers sprayed with scarlet, striped tubers of blackening copper. . . . And then he could see the porous, saffron liver of a great animal, or else an artificial fire of mercury arabesques, wisps of thorns dripping sanguine, and finally a kind of chalice of flaccid mother-of-pearl. ... That chalice then looked to him like an urn, and he thought that among those rocks was inhumed Father Caspar's corpse. No longer visible, if the action of the water had covered it with coralline cartilage; but the corals, absorbing the terrestrial humors of that body, had assumed shapes of flowers and garden fruits. Perhaps in a little while he would recognize the poor old man transformed into an alien creature down here: the globe of the head made from a hairy coconut, two withered apples for the cheeks, eyes and eyelids turned into two unripe apricots, the nose of sow thistle knotty like an animal's dung; below, in place of lips, dried figs, a beet with its apiculate stalk for the chin, and a wrinkled cardoon functioning as the throat; and at both temples, two chestnut burrs to act as sidecurls, and for ears the halves of a split walnut; for fingers, carrots; a watermelon as belly; quinces, the knees.[16]

Lists of Things, Persons, and Places

The history of literature is full of obsessive collections of objects. Sometimes these are fantastic, such as the things that, according to Ariosto, were found on the moon by Astolfo, who had gone there to retrieve Orlando's wits. Sometimes they are disturbing, such as the list of malign substances used by the

witches in Act 4 of *Macbeth.* Sometimes they are ec-
stasies of perfumes, such as the collection of flowers that Giambattista Marino describes in his *Adonis*
(Part 6, 115–159). Sometimes they are paltry but essential, such as the collection of flotsam that enables
Robinson Crusoe to survive on his island, or the
humble little treasure that Mark Twain tells us Tom
Sawyer put together. Sometimes they are dizzyingly
normal, such as the huge collection of insignificant
objects in Leopold Bloom's kitchen. Sometimes they
are poignant, despite a museum-like, almost funereal
immobility, such as the collection of musical instruments described by Thomas Mann in Chapter 7 of
Doctor Faustus.

The same holds true for places. Here again, the
writers rely on the *etcetera* of the list. Ezekiel 27 pro-
vides a list of properties to give an idea of the great-
ness of Tyre. Dickens, in the first chapter of *Bleak
House,* takes pains to show a London with features
made invisible by the smog that dominates the city.
Poe, in "The Man of the Crowd," trains his visionary
gaze on a series of individuals that he perceives com-
pactly as a "crowd." Proust (*Du côté de chez Swann,*
Chapter 3) summons up the city of his childhood.
Calvino (*Invisible Cities,* Chapter 9) evokes the cities
dreamed of by the Great Khan. Blaise Cendrars *(La
Prose du Transsibérien)* portrays the chugging of a

train across the Siberian steppes, through the recollection of various places. Whitman—celebrated as the poet who excelled, and was the most excessive, at composing vertiginous lists—piled objects atop one another to celebrate his native country:

> The axe leaps!
> The solid forest gives fluid utterances,
> They tumble forth, they rise and form,
> Hut, tent, landing, survey,
> Flail, plough, pick, crowbar, spade,
> Shingle, rail, prop, wainscot, lamb, lath, panel, gable,
> Citadel, ceiling, saloon, academy, organ, exhibition-
>   house, library,
> Cornice, trellis, pilaster, balcony, window, turret, porch,
> Hoe, rake, pitchfork, pencil, wagon, staff, saw, jack-
>   plane, mallet, wedge, rounce,
> Chair, tub, hoop, table, wicket, vane, sash, floor,
> Work-box, chest, string'd instrument, boat, frame, and
>   what not,
> Capitols of States, and capitol of the nation of States,
> Long stately rows in avenues, hospitals for orphans or
>   for the poor or sick,
> Manhattan steamboats and clippers taking the mea-
>   sure of all seas.[17]

Regarding the accumulation of places, in Hugo's *Ninety-Three* (Part 1, Chapter 3) there is a singular list of localities in the Vendée that the marquis de

Lantenac communicates orally to the sailor Halmalo, so he may pass through them all bearing the order for insurrection. It's obvious that poor Halmalo could never remember that huge list, and Hugo certainly doesn't expect the reader to remember it either. The immensity of the list of place names is intended simply to suggest the immensity of the popular rebellion.

Another dizzying list of places is brought into play by Joyce in the chapter of *Finnegans Wake* called "Anna Livia Plurabelle," where, to give a sense of the flowing of the River Liffey, Joyce inserted hundreds of river names from all over the world, disguised as puns or portmanteau words. It is not easy for the reader to recognize virtually unknown rivers in names such as the Chebb, Futt, Bann, Duck, Sabrainn, Till, Waag, Bomu, Boyana, Chu, Batha, Skollis, Shari, Sui, Tom, Chef, Syr Darya, Ladder Burn, and so on. Since translations of "Anna Livia" are usually quite free, a reference to a particular river might, in a foreign-language edition, appear in a location different from its place in the original text, or might even be altered completely. In the first Italian translation, made with the collaboration of Joyce himself, there are references to Italian rivers such as the Serio, Po, Serchio, Piave, Conca, Aniene, Ombrone, Lambro, Taro, Toce, Belbo, Sillaro, Tagliamento, Lamone, Brembo, Trebbio, Mincio, Tidone, and Panaro—none of which exist in the English text.[18] The same thing happened with the first, historic French translation.[19]

This list gives the impression of being potentially infinite. Not only must the reader make an effort to identify all the rivers, but one suspects that the critics have identified more rivers than those Joyce explicitly mentions. And one suspects, too, that as a consequence of the combinatorial possibilities offered by the English alphabet, there may be far more than either the critics or Joyce thought of.

This kind of list is difficult to classify. It stems from voraciousness, from the topos of ineffability (no one can say how many rivers there are in the world), and from a pure love of lists. Joyce must have toiled long and hard to find all those river names, enlisting the collaboration of many people. He certainly didn't do this out of a passion for geography. It's likely that he just did not want the list to have an end.

Ultimately, we glimpse the place of places: the entire universe. Borges, in his story "The Aleph," views it through a small crevice and sees it as a list that is destined to be incomplete—a list of places, people, and disquieting epiphanies. He sees the teeming ocean, dawn and dusk, the multitudes of the Americas, a silvery spiderweb at the center of a black pyramid, a broken labyrinth (which turns out to be London), an endless series of eyes viewed in closeup, all the mirrors on the planet, a rear courtyard on the Calle Soler displaying the same tiles he saw twenty years before in the entryway of a house in Fray Bentos, clusters of grapes, snow, tobacco, veins of metal, water vapor, convex equatorial deserts and their every grain of sand, a woman in Inverness, her tangled hair, her proud body, a cancer in her breast, a circle of dry soil in a sidewalk where there had once been a tree, a country house in Adrogué, a copy of the first English translation of Pliny, every letter of every page at once, simultaneous night and day, a sunset in Querétaro that seems to reflect the color of a rose in Bengal, his own empty bedroom, a study in Alkmaar containing a globe of the terraqueous world placed between two mirrors that multiply it endlessly, horses with wind-whipped manes on a shore of the Caspian Sea at dawn, the delicate bones of a hand, the survivors of a battle sending postcards, a Tarot card in a shop-window in Mirzapur, the oblique shadows of ferns on the floor of a greenhouse, tigers, pistons, bisons, tides, and armies, all the ants on earth, a Persian astrolabe, a desk drawer holding obscene, incredible, detailed letters written by his adored friend Beatriz Viterbo, a beloved monument in Chacarita Cemetery, the rotted remains of what had once, deliciously, been Beatriz, the circulation of his own dark blood, the coils and springs of love and the alterations of death. He sees the Aleph —one of the points in space that contains all other points—from everywhere at once, the earth in the Aleph, and the Aleph once more in the earth, and the earth in the Aleph. He gazes at his own face and his own viscera, and feels dizzy, and weeps, because his eyes have seen that secret, hypothetical object whose name has been usurped by men but which no man has ever truly looked upon: the inconceivable universe.[20]

I have always been fascinated by such lists—and I think I am in good company. It was certainly under Borges's influence that I tried, in *Baudolino,* to compose an imaginary geography. Baudolino is describing the marvels of the West to Prester John's son, a leper who faces certain death from his disease and who lives in seclusion, in a legendary Far Eastern country. Thus, he tells about the places and things of the Western world in the same fabulous way that the Western medieval world dreamed about the Far East:

I described the places I had seen, from Ratisbon to Paris, from Venice to Byzantium, and then Iconium and Armenia, and the peoples we had encountered on our journey. He was fated to die without having seen anything but the caves of Pndapetzim, so I tried to make him live through my tales. And I may also have invented: I spoke to him of cities I had never visited, of battles I had never fought, of princesses I had never possessed. I told him of the wonders of the lands where the sun dies. I made him enjoy the sunsets on the Propontis, the emerald glints on the Venetian lagoon, the valley in Hibernia where seven white churches lie on the shores of a silent lake; I told him how the Alps are covered with a soft white substance that in summer dissolves into majestic cataracts and is dispersed in rivers and streams along slopes rich in chestnut trees; I told him of the salt deserts that extend along the coasts of Apulia; I made him shiver as I described seas I had never sailed, where fish leap as big as calves, so tame that men can ride them; I reported the voyages of Saint Brendan to the Isles of the Blest, and how one day, believing he had reached a land in the midst of the sea, he descended on the back of a whale, which is a fish the size of a mountain, capable of swallowing a whole ship, but I had to explain to him what ships were, fish made of wood that cleave the waves, while moving white wings; I listed for him the wondrous animals of my country, the stag, who has two great horns in the form of a cross, the stork, who flies from one land to another, and takes care of its own parents when they are old, bearing them on its back through the skies, and the ladybug, which is like a small mushroom, red and dotted with milk-colored spots, the lizard, which is like a crocodile, but so small it can pass beneath a door, the cuckoo, who lays her eggs in the nests of other birds, the owl, whose round eyes in the night seem two lamps and who lives eating the oil of lamps in churches; the hedgehog, its back covered with sharp quills who sucks the milk of cows, the oyster, a living jewel box that sometimes produces a beauty which is dead but of inestimable value, the nightingale that keeps vigil singing and lives worshiping the rose, the lobster, a loricate monster of a flame-red color, who flees backwards to escape the hunters who dote on its flesh, the eel, frightful aquatic serpent with a fatty, exquisite flavor, the seagull that flies over the waters as if it were an angel of the Lord, but emits shrill cries like a devil, the blackbird, with yellow beak, that talks like a human, a sycophant repeating the confidences of its master, the swan that regally parts the water of a lake and sings at the moment of its death a very sweet melody, the weasel, sinuous as a maiden, the falcon that dives on its prey and carries it back to the knight who has trained it. I imagined the splendor of gems that he had never seen —nor had I—the purplish and milky patches of murrhine, the flushed and white veins of certain Egyptian stones, the whiteness of orichalc, transparent crystal, brilliant diamond; and then I sang the praises of the splendor of gold, a soft metal that can be transformed into the finest leaf, the hiss of the red-hot slivers when they are plunged into water to be tempered, and the unimaginable reliquaries to be seen in the treasures of the great abbeys, the high and pointed spires of our churches, the high and straight columns of the Hippodrome of Constantinople, the books the Jews read, scattered with signs that seem insects, and the sounds they produce when they read them, and how a great Christian king had received from a caliph an iron cock that sang alone at every sunrise, then what a sphere is that turns while belching steam, and how the mirrors of Archimedes burn, how frightening it is to see a windmill at night, and I told him also of the Grasal, of the knights still searching for it in Brittany, about ourselves and how we would give it to his father as soon as we found the unspeakable Zosimos. Seeing that these splendors fascinated him, but their inaccessibility saddened him, I thought it was good to convince him that his suffering was not the worst, to tell him of the torment of Andronicus with such details that they far surpassed what had been done to him, of the massacres of Crema, of prisoners with a hand, an ear, the nose cut off; I brought before his eyes images of indescribable maladies compared to which leprosy was the lesser evil; I told him how horrendously horrible were scrofula, erysipelas, St. Vitus' dance, shingles, the bite of the tarantula, scabies, which makes you scratch your skin, scale by scale, and the pestiferous action of the asp, the torture of Saint Agatha, whose breasts were torn away, and that of Saint Lucy, whose eyes were gouged out, and of Saint Sebastian, pierced by arrows, of Saint Stephen, his skull shattered by stones, of Saint Lawrence, roasted on a grill over a slow fire, and I invented other saints and other atrocities, such as Saint Ursicinus, impaled from the anus to the mouth, Saint Sarapion, flayed, Saint Mopsuestius, his four limbs bound to four horses, crazed and then quartered, Saint Dracontius, forced to swallow boiling pitch. . . . It seemed to me these horrors brought him some relief, but then I feared I had gone too far and I began describing the world's other beauties, often a solace of prisoner's thoughts: the grace of Parisian girls, the lazy opulence of Venetian prostitutes, the incomparable complexion of an empress, the childish laugh of Colandrina, the eyes of a far-off princess. He became excited, asked me to tell him more, wanted to know what the hair was like of Melisenda, countess of Tripoli, the lips of those abundant beauties who had enchanted the knights of Broceliande more than the Holy Grasal itself. He became excited; God forgive me, I believe that once or twice he had an erection and felt the pleasure of casting his seed. And more, I tried to make him understand how the universe was rich in spices with languid scents, and, since I had none with me, I tried to recall the names of both the spices I had known and those I had only heard of, words that would intoxicate him like perfumes, and for him I listed malabaster, incense, nard, lycium, sandal, saffron, ginger, cardamom, senna, zedoaria, laurel, marjoram, coriander, dill, thyme, clove, sesame, poppy, nutmeg, citronella, curcuma, and cumin. The deacon listened, on the threshold of delirium, touched his face as if his poor nose could not bear all those fragrances; he asked, weeping, what they had given him to eat till now, those accursed eunuchs, on the pretext that he was ill, goat's milk and bread soaked in burq, which they said was good for leprosy, and he spent his days stunned, almost always sleeping and with the same taste in his mouth, day after day.[21]

Wunderkammern and Museums

A museum catalogue is an example of a practical list which refers to objects that exist in a predetermined place, and, as such, it is necessarily finite. But how should we consider a museum *in se*, or any kind of collection? Except for extremely rare cases of collections that contain *all* the objects of a certain type (for example, all—and I mean all—the works of a given artist), a collection is always open and could always be increased with the addition of some other element, especially if the collection is based—as one could say of the collections of Roman patricians, medieval lords, and modern museums—on a taste for accumulation and increase *ad infinitum*. Though a museum might display a great quantity of works of art, it gives the impression that they are even more numerous than that.

What's more, save for highly specialized cases, collections always verge on the incongruous. A space traveler unaware of our concept of art would wonder why the Louvre contains trifles in common use such as vases, plates, or salt shakers, statues of a goddess such as the Venus de Milo, representations of landscapes, portraits of normal people, tomb artifacts and mummies, portrayals of monstrous creatures, objects of worship, images of human beings suffering torture, paintings of battles, nudes calculated to arouse sexual desire, and archaeological finds.

Because the objects are so varied, and because one imagines what it would be like to be surrounded by them at night, a museum can be a terrifying experience. And the sense of uneasiness grows with the quantity and incongruity of the collected objects.

When the collected objects are unrecognizable, even a modern museum can resemble the seventeenth- and eighteenth-century forerunners of our natural-science museums: the so-called *Wunderkammern*—"wonder cabinets," or "cabinets of curiosities"—where some people tried to amass systematic collections of all the things that ought to be known, while others collected things that seemed extraordinary or unheard of, including bizarre objects or amazing items such as a stuffed crocodile, which was usually hung from a keystone dominating the entire room. In many of these collections, such as the one put together by Peter the Great in St. Petersburg, deformed fetuses were carefully preserved in spirits.

The waxworks in the Museo della Specola in Florence present a collection of anatomical marvels, hyperrealistic masterpieces of bodies eviscerated and laid bare, in a symphony of tones ranging from pink to dark red, and thence down to the browns of intestines, livers, lungs, stomachs, and spleens.

What remains of the *Wunderkammern* consists largely of the pictorial representations or etchings in their catalogues. Some were made up of hundreds of little shelves holding stones, shells, the skeletons of unusual animals, and masterpieces of the taxidermist's art, which was capable of creating nonexistent animals. Other *Wunderkammern* were like museums in miniature—cupboards divided into compartments containing items that, divorced from their original context, seem to tell senseless or incongruous stories.

From illustrated catalogues such as the *Museum Celeberrimum,* by de Sepibus (1678), and the *Museum Kircherianum,* by Bonanni (1709), we learn that in the collection put together by Father Athanasius Kircher at the Roman College, there were ancient statues, pagan cult objects, amulets, Chinese idols, votive tables, two tablets showing the fifty incarnations of Brahma, Roman tomb inscriptions, lanterns, rings, seals, buckles, armillas, weights, bells, stones and fossils with strange images engraved by Nature on their surface, exotic objects *ex variis orbis plagis collectum,* containing the belts of Brazilian natives adorned with the teeth of devoured victims, exotic birds and other stuffed animals, a book from Malabar made of palm leaves, Turkish artifacts, Chinese scales, barbarian weapons, Indian fruits, the foot of an Egyptian mummy, fetuses from forty days old to seven months old, skeletons of eagles, hoopoes, magpies, thrushes, Brazilian monkeys, cats and mice, moles, porcupines, frogs, chameleons, and sharks, as well as marine plants, a seal's tooth, a crocodile, an armadillo, a tarantula, a hippo's head, a rhinoceros horn, a monstrous dog in a vase preserved in a balsamic solution, giants' bones, musical and mathematical instruments, experimental projects on perpetual motion, automatons and other devices along the lines of the machines made by Archimedes and Heron of Alexandria, cochleas, an octagonal catoptric device that multiplied a little model elephant so that "it restores the image of a herd of elephants that seemed to have been collected from all of Asia and Africa," hydraulic machines, telescopes and microscopes with microscopic observations of insects, globes, armillary spheres, astrolabes, planispheres, solar, hydraulic, mechanical, and magnetic clocks, lenses, hourglasses, instruments for measuring temperature and humidity, various paintings and images of mountains and precipices, winding channels in valleys, wooded labyrinths, foaming waves, whirlpools, hills, architectural perspectives, ruins, ancient monuments, battles, massacres, duels, triumphs, palaces, biblical mysteries, and effigies of gods.

I greatly enjoyed imagining one of the characters in *Foucault's Pendulum* wandering through the deserted corridors of the Conservatoire des Arts et Métiers in Paris—a museum of the history of technology which contains obsolete mechanisms whose function is no longer clear to visitors, so that the whole Conservatoire looks like a Baroque *Wunderkammer.* It increases the visitor's impression of being menaced by unknown artificial monsters, and sets off in his hallucinating mind an uninterrupted series of paranoid fantasies:

On the floor stretches a line of vehicles: bicycles, horseless carriages, automobiles; from the ceiling hang planes. Some of the objects are intact, though peeling and corroded by time, and in the ambiguous mix of natural and electric light they seem covered by a patina, an old violin's varnish. Others are only skeletons or chassis, rods and cranks that threaten indescribable tortures. You picture yourself chained to a rack, something digging into your flesh until you confess.

Beyond this sequence of antique machines—once

mobile, now immobile, their souls rusted, mere specimens of the technological pride that is so keen to display them to the reverence of visitors—stands the choir,
guarded on the left by a scale model of the Statue of
Liberty that Bartholdi designed for another world, and
on the right by a statue of Pascal. Here the swaying
Pendulum is flanked by the nightmare of a deranged
entomologist—chelae, mandibles, antennae, proglotti-
des, and wings—a cemetery of mechanical corpses that
look as if they might all start working again at any moment—magnetos, monophase transformers, turbines,
converters, steam engines, dynamos. In the rear, in the
ambulatory beyond the Pendulum, rest Assyrian idols,
and Chaldean, Carthaginian, great Baals whose bellies,
long ago, glowed red-hot, and Nuremberg Maidens
whose hearts still bristle with naked nails: these were
once airplane engines. Now they form a horrible gar-
land of simulacra that lie in adoration of the Pendulum; it is as if the progeny of Reason and the Enlight-
enment had been condemned to stand guard forever
over the ultimate symbol of Tradition and Wisdom.

. . . . .

Go downstairs. Move. . . . For hours I had waited
for this, but now that it was possible, even wise, to
do it, I felt somehow paralyzed. I would have to cross
the rooms at night, using my flashlight only when necessary. The barest hint of a nocturnal glow filtered
through the big windows. I had imagined a museum
made ghostly by the moon's rays; I was wrong. The
glass cases reflected vague glints from outside; that was

all. If I didn't move carefully, I could go sprawling on the floor, could knock over something with a shatter of glass, a clang of metal. Now and then I turned on the flashlight, turned it off. Proceeding, I felt as if I were at the Crazy Horse. The sudden beam revealed a nakedness, not of flesh, but of screws, clamps, rivets.

What if I were suddenly to reveal a living presence, the figure of an envoy of the Masters echoing, mirroring my progress? Who would be the first to shout? I listened. In vain. Gliding, I made no noise. Neither did he.

That afternoon I had studied carefully the sequence of the rooms, in order to be able to find the great staircase even in darkness. But instead I was wandering, groping. I had lost my bearings.

Perhaps I was going in circles, crossing some of the rooms for the second time; perhaps I would never get out of this place; perhaps this groping among meaningless machines was the rite.

. . . . .

Froment's Motor: a vertical structure on a rhomboid base. It enclosed, like an anatomical figure exhibiting its ribs and viscera, a series of reels, batteries, circuit breakers—what the hell did the textbooks call them?—and the thing was driven by a transmission belt fed by a toothed wheel. . . . What could it have been used for? Answer: for measuring the telluric currents, of course.

Accumulators. What did they accumulate? I imagined the Thirty-six Invisibles as stubborn secretaries (keepers of the secret) tapping all night on their clavier-scribes to produce from this machine a sound, a spark, all of them intent on a dialogue from coast to coast, from abyss to surface, from Machu Picchu to Avalon, come in, come in, hello hello hello, Pamersiel Pamersiel, we've caught a tremor, current Mu 36, the one the Brahmans worshiped as the breath of God, now I'll plug in the tap, the valve, all micro-macrocosmic circuits operational, all the mandrake roots shuddering beneath the crust of the globe, you hear the song of the Universal Sympathetic, over and out.

. . . . .

And as they operated these pseudothermic hexa-tetragrammatic electrocapillatories—that's how Garamond would have put it—every now and then someone would invent, say, a vaccine or an electric bulb, a triumph in the wonderful adventure of metals, but the real task was quite different: here they are, assembled at midnight, to spin this static-electricity machine of Ducretet, a transparent wheel that looks like a bandoleer, and, inside it, two little vibrating balls supported by arched sticks, and when they touch, sparks fly, and Dr. Frankenstein hopes to give life to his golem, but no, the signal has another purpose: Dig, dig, old mole. . . .

A sewing machine (what else? One of those engraving-advertisements, along with pills for developing one's bust, and the great eagle flying over the mountains with the restorative cordial in its talons, Robur le Conquérant, R.C.), but when you turn it on,

it turns a wheel, and the wheel turns a coil, and the coil.
. . . What does the coil do? Who is listening to the coil?
The label says, "Currents induced from the terrestrial
field." Shameless! There to be read even by children on
their afternoon visits! . . .

I passed by. I imagined myself dwindling, an ant-
sized, dazed pedestrian in the streets of a mechanical
city, metallic skyscrapers on every side. Cylinders, batteries, Leyden jars one above the other, merry-go-
round centrifuges, tourniquet électrique à attraction et
répulsion, a talisman to stimulate the sympathetic currents, colonnade étincelante formée de neuf tubes,
électroaimant, a guillotine, and in the center—it looked
like a printing press—hooks hung from chains, the
kind you might see in a stable. A press in which you
could crush a hand, a head. A glass bell with a pneu-
matic pump, two-cylinder, a kind of alembic, with a
cup underneath and, to the right, a copper sphere. In it
Saint-Germain concocted his dyes for the landgrave of
Hesse.

A pipe rack with two rows of little hourglasses, ten
to a row, their necks elongated like the neck of a Mo-
digliani woman, some unspecified material inside, and
the upper bulge of each expanded to a different size,
like balloons about to take off. This, an apparatus for
the production of the Rebis, where anyone could see it.

Then the glassworks section. I had retraced my
steps. Little green bottles: a sadist host offering me
poisons in quintessence. Iron machines for making

bottles, opened and closed by two cranks. What if, instead of a bottle, someone put a wrist in there? Whack! And it would be the same with those great pincers, those immense scissors, those curved scalpels that could be inserted into sphincters or ears, into the uterus to extract the still-living fetus, which would be ground with honey and pepper to sate the appetite of Astarte. . . . The room I was now crossing had broad cases, and buttons to set in motion corkscrews that would advance inexorably toward the victim's eye, the Pit and the Pendulum. We were close to caricature now, to the ridiculous contraptions of Rube Goldberg, the torture racks on which Big Pete bound Mickey Mouse, the engrenage extérieur à trois pignons, triumph of Renaissance mechanics, Branca, Ramelli, Zonca. . . . All ready, these instruments awaited a sign, everything in full view, the Plan was public, but nobody could have guessed it, the creaking mechanical maws would sing their hymn of conquest, great orgy of mouths, all teeth that locked and meshed exactly, mouths singing in tick-tock spasms.

Finally I came to the émetteur à étincelles soufflées designed for the Eiffel Tower, for the emission of time signals between France, Tunisia, and Russia, the Templars of Provins, the Paulicians, the Assassins of Fez. (Fez isn't in Tunisia, and the Assassins, anyway, were in Persia, but you can't split hairs when you live in the coils of Transcendent Time.) I had seen it before, this immense machine, taller than I, its walls perforated by a series of portholes, air ducts. The sign said it was a radio apparatus, but I knew better, I had passed it that same afternoon. The Beaubourg!

For all to see. And, for that matter, what was the real purpose of that enormous box in the center of Lutetia (Lutetia, the air duct in a subterranean sea of mud), where once there was the Belly of Paris, with those prehensile proboscises of vents, that insanity of pipes, conduits, that Ear of Dionysius open to the sky to capture sounds, messages, signals, and send them to the very center of the globe, and then to return them, vomiting out information from hell? First the Conservatoire, a laboratory, then the Tower, a probe, and finally the Beaubourg, a global transmitter and receiver. Had they set up that huge suction cup just to entertain a handful of hairy, smelly students, who went there to listen to the latest record with a Japanese headset? For all to see. The Beaubourg, gate to the underground kingdom of Agarttha, the monument of the Resurgentes Equites Synarchici. And the rest—two, three, four billion of them—were unaware of this, or forced themselves to look the other way.[22]

Definition by List of Properties versus Definition by Essence

Homer describes the shield as a form because he knows exactly how life in that society works; he merely lists the warriors because he does not know how many there are. Thus, one might think that forms would be characteristic of mature cultures, which know the world they have succeeded in exploring and defining, while lists would be typical of primitive cultures that still have an imprecise image of the universe and try to itemize as many of its properties as they can, without establishing a hierarchical relationship among them. We will see that according to a certain profile, this can be true—yet the list turns up again in the Middle Ages (when the great theological *Summae* and the encyclopedias claimed to provide a definitive form for the material and spiritual universe), in the Renaissance and the Baroque period (when the form of the world was that of a new astronomy), and especially in the modern and postmodern world. Let us reflect on the first part of the problem.

The dream of every philosophy and science, from the days of ancient Greece onward, has been to know and define things by *essence.* Beginning with Aristotle, definition by essence has meant defining a given thing as an individual of a given species, and the species in turn as a member of a given genus.[23] This is the same procedure followed by modern taxonomy when it defines animals and plants. Naturally, the system of classes and subclasses is more complex. For example, a tiger belongs to the species *Tigris,* genus *Panthera,* family *Felidae,* suborder *Fissipedia,* order *Carnivora,* subclass *Eutheria,* and class *Mammalia.*

A platypus is a species of monotreme (egg-laying) mammal. But after the platypus was discovered, eighty years passed before it was defined as a monotreme mammal. During that time, scientists had to decide how to classify it; and until they did, it remained, rather disturbingly, a creature the size of a mole, with little eyes, a duck's bill, a tail, paws that it used for swimming and for digging burrows, the front paws having four claws joined by a membrane (a membrane bigger than the one joining the claws of the hind paws), the capacity to produce eggs, and the ability to feed its young with milk from its mammary glands.

This is exactly what nonspecialists would say when looking at a platypus. Note that by referring to this disordered set of properties, nonspecialists would be able to tell a platypus from an ox, whereas if they—knowing nothing about scientific taxonomy—were told that it was a "monotreme mammal," they would not be able to tell a platypus from a kangaroo. If a child asks his mother what a tiger is and what it's like, she would be unlikely to reply that it is a mammal of the suborder *Fissipedia* or a fissiped carnivore, but would probably say that it is a ferocious wild beast that looks like a cat but is bigger, very agile, yellow with black stripes, lives in the jungle, is occasionally a man-eater, and so on.

A definition by essence takes substances into consideration, and we presume we know the entire gamut of substances—for example, "living being," "animal," "plant," "mineral." In contrast, according to Aristotle, a definition by properties is a definition by accidents, and accidents are infinite in number. A tiger—which according to definition by essence is a member of the kingdom *Animalia,* phylum *Chordata*—is characterized by a number of species-wide properties: it has four legs, looks like a big cat, is striped, weighs an average of so many pounds, roars in a typical way, and has an average lifespan of so many years. But a tiger could also be an animal that was in Rome's Coliseum on a particular day in Nero's time, or that was killed on May 24, 1846, by an English military officer named Ferguson, or that has myriad other accidental traits.

The reality is that we seldom define things by essence; more often, we give lists of properties. And this is why all the lists that define something through a nonfinite series of properties, even though apparently vertiginous, seem to be closer to the way in which, in everyday life (though not in academic science departments), we define and recognize things.[24] A representation by accumulation or series of properties presupposes not a dictionary, but a kind of encyclopedia—one which is never finished, and which the members of a given culture know and master, according to their competence, only in part.

We use descriptions via properties when we belong to a primitive culture that has yet to construct a hierarchy of genera and species, and that doesn't have definitions by essence. But this can also be true of a mature culture that is dissatisfied with some existing essential definitions and wants to call them into question, or that tries, by discovering new properties, to increase the store of knowledge about particular items in its encyclopedia.

The Italian rhetorician Emanuele Tesauro, in *Il Cannocchiale aristotelico,* or *The Aristotelian Telescope* (1665), proposes the model of the metaphor as a way to discover hitherto unknown relationships between known data. The method works by compiling a repertoire of known things that the metaphoric imagination can use to find new parallels, links, and affinities. In this way, Tesauro formulates the idea of a Categorical Index—which looks like an enormous dictionary but is in fact a series of accidental properties. He presents his index (with Baroque delight in such a "marvelous" idea) as a "truly secret secret," an essential tool for "revealing objects that are hidden within various categories and for making comparisons between them." In other words, it has the capacity to unearth analogies and similarities that would have gone unnoticed if everything had remained classified in its own category.

Here, I can do little more than provide a few examples from Tesauro's catalogue, which seems capable of endless expansion. His list of "Substances" is completely open-ended, comprising Divine Persons, Ideas, Gods of Fable, Angels, Demons, and Spirits; under "Heavens," he includes Wandering Stars, the Zodiac, Vapors, Exhalations, Meteors, Comets, Lightning, and the Winds; the category "Earth" comprises Fields, Wildernesses, Mountains, Hills, and Promontories; that of "Bodies" includes Stones, Gems, Metals, and Grasses; "Mathematics" includes Globes, Compasses, Squares, and so on. Likewise in the category "Quantities": under "Quantity of Volume" we find the Small, the Great, the Long, and the Short; under "Quantity of Weight," the Light and the Heavy. In the category "Quality," under "Seeing" we find the Visible and the Invisible, the Apparent, the Beautiful and the Deformed, the Clear and the Obscure, Black and White; under "Smell" we find Aroma and Stink—and so on with the categories of "Relation," "Action and Affection," "Position," "Time," "Place," and "State." To take one example, under the category "Quantity," subcategory "Quantity of Volume," subsubcategory "Small Things," one can find angels who stand on the head of a pin, incorporeal forms, the poles as the motionless points on a sphere, zenith and nadir. Among "Elementary Things," we find the spark of fire, the drop of water, the scruple of stone, the grain of sand, the gem, and the atom; among "Human Things," the embryo, the abortus, the pygmy, and the dwarf; among "Animals," the ant and the flea; among "Plants," the mustard seed and the breadcrumb; among "Sciences," the mathematical point; under "Architecture," the tip of the pyramid.

This list seems to have neither rhyme nor reason, like all Baroque attempts to encapsulate the global content of a body of knowledge. In *Technica curiosa* (1664) and his book on natural magic, *Joco-seriorium naturae et artis sive magiae naturalis centuriae tres* (1665), Caspar Schott mentions a work, written in 1653, whose author presented in Rome an *Artificium* comprising forty-four fundamental classes: Elements (fire, wind, smoke, ash, hell, purgatory, the center of the Earth), Heavenly Entities (stars, lightning, rainbow), Intellectual Entities (God, Jesus, discourse, opinion, suspicion, soul, stratagem, or specter), Secular States (emperors, barons, plebeians), Ecclesiastical States, Craftsmen (painters, sailors),

Instruments, Affections (love, justice, lust), Religion, Sacramental Confession, Tribunal, Army, Medicine (doctors, hunger, enema), Brute Beasts, Birds, Reptiles, Fish, Parts of Animals, Furnishings, Foods, Drinks and Liquids (wine, beer, water, butter, wax, resin), Clothing, Silk Fabrics, Wools, Canvas and Other Woven Fabrics, Nautical (ship, anchor), Aromas (cinnamon, chocolate), Metals, Coins, Various Artifacts, Stones, Jewels, Trees, Fruits, Public Places, Weights, Measures, Numerals, Time, Adjectives, Adverbs, Prepositions, Persons (pronouns, titles such as "His Eminence the Cardinal"), Traveling (hay, road, robber).

I could go on by quoting other Baroque lists, ranging from Kircher to Wilkins, each more dizzying than the next. In all of them, the lack of a systematic spirit testifies to the effort made by the encyclopedist to elude obsolete classifications by genera and species.[25]

Excess

From a literary point of view, such "scientific" attempts at classification offered to writers a model of *prodigality*, though one could say that, on the contrary, it was the writers who were offering the model to the scientists. Indeed, one of the early masters of the runaway list was Rabelais, and he used such lists precisely in order to subvert the rigid order of the medieval academic *Summae*.

At this point, the list—which in classical times had been almost a *pis aller,* a last resort, a way to speak of the inexpressible when words failed, a tortured catalogue which implied the silent hope of finding, eventually, a form that would impose order on a bunch of random accidents—became a poetic act performed for the pure love of *deformation.* Rabelais initiated a poetics of the list for the list, a poetics of the list by *excess.*

Only a taste for excess could have inspired the Baroque fabulist Giambattista Basile, in his *Tale of Tales, or The Entertainment for Little Ones*—when telling of how seven brothers are turned into seven doves because of their sister's misdeed—to expand his text with a great flock of bird names: kites, hawks, falcons, water-hens, snipes, goldfinches, woodpeckers, jays, owls, magpies, jackdaws, rooks, starlings, woodcocks, cocks, hens and chickens, turkey-cocks, blackbirds, thrushes, chaffinches, tomtits, jennywrens, lapwings, linnets, greenfinches, crossbills, flycatchers, larks, plovers, kingfishers, wagtails, redbreasts, redfinches, sparrows, ducks, fieldfares, woodpigeons, bullfinches. It was for love of excess that Robert Burton, in his *Anatomy of Melancholy* (Book 2,

Part 2), described an ugly woman by accumulating, over pages and pages, an outrageous number of pejoratives and insults. And it was love of excess that led Giambattista Marino, in Part 10 of his *Adonis,* to produce a deluge of lines on the fruits of human artifice: "astrolabes and almanacs, traps, rasps and picklocks, cages, bedlam, tabards, shell cases and sacks, labyrinths, plumb-rules and levels, dice, cards, ball, board and chessmen and rattles and pulleys and gimlets, reels, winders, parrels, clocks, alembics, decanters, bellows and crucibles, look, bags and blisters full of wind, and swollen bubbles of soap, towers of smoke, nettle leaves, pumpkin flowers, green and yellow feathers, spiders, scarabs, crickets, ants, wasps, mosquitoes, fireflies and moths, mice, cats, silkworms, and a hundred such extravaganzas of devices and animals; all these you see and other strange phantasms again in massive ranks."[26]

It is out of a taste for excess that Victor Hugo, in *Ninety-Three* (Book 2, Chapter 3), when suggesting the mammoth dimensions of the Republican Convention, explodes in page after page of names, so that what might be an archival register becomes a mind-boggling experience. The very list of excessive and extravagant lists could itself become extravagant and excessive.

Unrestraint does not mean incongruity: a list can

be excessive (see, for instance, the catalogue of the games played by Gargantua) yet also fully coherent (that list of games is a logical enumeration of pastimes). So there are lists which are *coherent in their excess* and others which are not excessively long but which represent an assemblage of things deliberately devoid of any apparent interrelation—so much so, that such cases are referred to as instances of *chaotic enumeration.*[27]

Perhaps the best example of a successful blend of immoderation and coherence is the description of the flowers in the garden of Paradou in the novel *La Faute de l'Abbé Mouret,* or *Abbé Mouret's Transgression,* by Zola. A completely chaotic example might be the enumeration of names and things compiled by Cole Porter in his song "You're the Top!": the Coliseum, the Louvre Museum, a melody from a symphony by Strauss, a Bendel bonnet, a Shakespeare sonnet, Mickey Mouse, the Nile, the Tower of Pisa, the smile on the Mona Lisa, Mahatma Gandhi, Napoleon brandy, the purple light of a summer night in Spain, the National Gallery, cellophane, a turkey dinner, a Coolidge dollar, the nimble tread of the feet of Fred Astaire, an O'Neill drama, Whistler's mama, camembert, a rose, Inferno's Dante, the nose on the great Durante, a dance in Bali, a hot tamale, an angel, a Botticelli, Keats, Shelley, Ovaltine, a boom, the moon over Mae West's shoulder, a Waldorf salad, a Berlin ballad, the boats that glide on the sleepy Zuider Zee, an old Dutch master, Lady Astor, broccoli, romance . . . Yet the list does acquire a certain coherence, since it mentions all the things that Porter believes are as wonderful as the person he loves. We can criticize the lack of discrimination in his list of values, but not his logic.

Chaotic enumeration is not the same as stream of consciousness. All the interior monologues in Joyce would be pure collections of entirely anomalous elements, were it not for the fact that, to make them a coherent whole, we assume they emerge from the consciousness of a single character, one after another, via associations that the author is not always obliged to explain.

Tyrone Slothrop's desk, described by Thomas Pynchon in the first chapter of *Gravity's Rainbow,* is certainly chaotic, but its description is not. The same is true for the description of the chaos in Bloom's kitchen, in *Ulysses.* It is hard to say whether the unrestrained list of the things that Georges Perec sees in a single day in the Place Saint-Sulpice in Paris (*Tentative d'épuisement d'un lieu parisien*) is coherent or chaotic. The list is bound to be random and disordered: the square, on that day, was no doubt the scene of a hundred thousand other events that Perec neither noticed nor wrote down. But on the other hand, the fact that the list contains only what he noticed makes it disconcertingly homogeneous.

Among lists that are excessive and coherent, we might also include the portrayal of the slaughterhouse in Alfred Döblin's novel *Berlin Alexanderplatz*. In principle, this passage should be the orderly description of a processing facility and the operations carried out in it; but the reader has difficulty perceiving the layout of the place and the logical sequence of activities, amid that dense agglomeration of details, numerical data, gouts of blood, and herds of frightened piglets. Döblin's abattoir is horrible because the mass of particulars is so overwhelming that it stuns the reader. Any possible order simply falls apart in the disorder of mad bestiality—which alludes prophetically to future slaughterhouses.

Döblin's description of the slaughterhouse is like Pynchon's depiction of Slothrop's desk: a nonchaotic representation of a chaotic situation. It was that kind of pseudo-chaotic list that inspired me when I was writing Chapter 28 of *Baudolino*.

Baudolino and his friends are heading toward the legendary land of Prester John. Suddenly, they come to the Sambatyon—the river that, according to rabbinic tradition, has no water in it. There is only a raging torrent of sand and stones, making a noise so deafening that it can be heard at a distance of a day's march. That stony flow ceases only at the beginning of the Sabbath, and only on the Sabbath can it be crossed.

I imagined that a river made of stones would be rather chaotic, especially if the stones were of different sizes, colors, and hardnesses. I found a marvelous list of stones and other minerals in Pliny's *Natural History;* the very names of those substances worked in concert to make the list more "musical." Here are some specimens from my catalogue:

> It was a majestic course of rocks and clods, flowing ceaselessly, and in that current of great shapeless masses could be discerned irregular slabs, sharp as blades, broad as tombstones, and between them, gravel, fossils, peaks, and crags. Moving at the same speed, as if driven by an impetuous wind, fragments of travertine rolled over and over, great faults sliding above; then, their impetus lessening, they bounced off streams of spall, while little chips, now round, smoothed as if by water in their sliding between boulder and boulder, leaped up, falling back with sharp sounds, to be caught in those same eddies they themselves had created, crashing and grinding. Amid and above this overlapping of mineral, puffs of sand were formed, gusts of chalk, clouds of lapilli, foams of pumice, rills of mire. Here and there sprays of shards, volleys of coals, fell on the bank, and the travelers had to cover their faces so as not to be scarred.

. . . . .

For two days they had seen above the horizon an impervious chain of high mountains, which loomed over the travelers, almost blocking their view of the sky, crammed as they were in an ever narrower passage, with no exit, from which, way, way above, could now be seen only a great cloud, barely luminescent, that gnawed the top of those peaks. Here, from a fissure, like a wound between two mountains, they saw the Sambatyon springing up: a roiling of sandstone, a gurgling of tuff, a dripping of muck, a ticking of shards, a grumbling of clotted earth, an overflowing of clods, a rain of clay, all gradually transformed into a steady flow, which began its journey towards some boundless ocean of sand. Our friends spent a day trying to skirt the mountains and discover a pass above the source, but in vain.

. . . . .

They decided to follow the river . . . until, after almost five days' travel, and nights as sultry as the days, they realized that the continuous churn of that tide was changing. The river had assumed a greater speed; in its flow something like currents were visible, rapids that dragged along shreds of basalt like straws, a distant thunder was heard. . . . Then, more and more impetuous, the Sambatyon subdivided into myriad streamlets, which penetrated among mountainous slopes like the fingers of a hand in a clump of mud; at times a wave was swallowed by a grotto, then, from a sort of rocky passage that seemed impassable, it emerged with a roar and flung itself angrily towards the valley. Abruptly, after a vast curve they were forced to make because the banks had become impervious, lashed by granite whirlwinds, the friends reached the top of a plateau, and saw the Sambatyon below them, annihilated in a sort of maw of Hell. There were cataracts that plunged down from dozens of rocky eaves arranged like an amphitheater, into a boundless final vortex, an incessant retching of granite, an eddy of bitumen, a sole undertow of alum, a churning of schist, a clash of orpiment against the banks. And on the matter that the vortex erupted towards the sky, but low with respect to the eyes of those who looked down as if from the top of a tower, the sun's rays formed on those silicious droplets an immense rainbow that, as every body reflected the rays with varying splendor according to its own nature, had many more colors than those usually formed in the sky after a storm, and, unlike them, seemed destined to shine eternally, never dissolving. It was a reddening of haematrites and cinnabars, a glow of blackness as if it were steel, a flight of crumbs of aureopigment from yellow to bright orange, a blueness of armenium, a whiteness of calcinated shells, a greening of malachite, a fading of liothargirium into saffrons ever paler, a blare of risigallam, a belching of greenish earth that faded into dust of crisocolla and then transmigrated into nuances of indigo and violet, a triumph of aurum musivum, a purpling of burnt white lead, a flaring of sandracca, a couch of silvered clay, a single transparence of alabaster. No human voice could make itself heard in that clangor, nor did the travelers have any desire to speak. They witnessed the death agony of the Sambatyon enraged at having to vanish into the bowels of the earth, trying to take with it all that surrounded it, clenching its stones to express all its impotence.[28]

There are lists that become chaotic through an excess of ire, hatred, and rancor, unleashing cascades of insults. A typical example is a passage in *Bagatelles pour un massacre,* where Céline bursts out in a flood of abuse—not against the Jews, for once, but against Soviet Russia:

Bing! Badabing! They're snuffing it! Bloated! By God's guts! . . . 487 million! Of impalificated cossackologists! Quid? Quid? Quod? In all the chancres of Slavonia! Quid! From the Slavigothic Baltic to the White Black Highseas? Quam? The Balkans! Slimy! Rotten as cucumbers! . . . Stinking shitspreaders! Of ratshit! I don't give a flying fart . . . I don't give a fuck! I'm out of here, bigtime! Cow pats! Immensely! Volgaronov! . . . Tataronesque Mushymongoloids! . . . Stakhanovicious! Arselikoff! Four hundred thousand versts . . . of shitcrusted steppe, of Zébis-Laridon hides! . . . I've come across the mother of all Vesuviuses here! Floods! . . . Fungus-infected arsewipes! . . . The Tsar's chamber pots for you and your filthy perverted arseholes! . . . Stabilin! Voroshitsky! Limpdick leftovers! . . . TransBeria!"[29]

Chaotic Enumeration

It seems impossible to define every enumeration as chaotic, since, from a certain point of view, any enumeration can acquire some coherence. There would be nothing incongruous even about a list that put together a broom, an incomplete copy of a biography of Galen, a fetus preserved in alcohol, and (to quote Lautréamont) an umbrella and a dissecting table. One would only have to establish that this was an inventory of objects relegated to the cellar of a medical school. A list which includes Jesus, Julius Caesar, Cicero, Louis IX, Raymond Lully, Joan of Arc, Gilles de Rais, Damiens, Lincoln, Hitler, Mussolini, Kennedy, and Saddam Hussein becomes a homogeneous collection if we note that all of these are people who did not die in their own bed.

To find examples of genuine chaotic enumeration, which anticipates the unsettling lists of the Surrealists, we should look at Rimbaud's poem "Le Bateau Ivre." In fact, à propos of Rimbaud, one scholar has proposed that there is a difference between *conjunctive* and *disjunctive* enumeration.[30] All of my previous quotations are examples of conjunctive enumeration: they each rely on a specific universe of discourse according to which the elements of the list acquire a certain mutual coherence. In contrast, disjunctive enumeration enacts a shattering, like the experience that afflicts a schizophrenic who becomes aware of a sequence of disparate impressions and is unable to impose any unity on them. Leo Spitzer was inspired by the notion of disjunctive enumeration when he formulated his concept of chaotic enumeration.[31] In fact he cited, by way of example, these verses from Rimbaud's *Illuminations*:

> In the woods there is a bird; his song stops you and
>   makes you blush.
> There is a clock that never strikes.
> There is a hollow with a nest of white beasts.
> There is a cathedral that goes down and a lake that
>   goes up.
> There is a little carriage abandoned in the copse or
>   that goes running down the road beribboned.
> There is a troupe of little actors in costume, glimpsed
>   on the road through the border of the woods.
> And then, when you are hungry and thirsty, there is
>   someone who drives you away.[32]

As for chaotic enumeration, literature offers a wealth of examples, from Pablo Neruda to Jacques Prévert, up to and including Calvino's *Cosmicomics*, which depicts the random formation of the Earth's surface by meteoric detritus. Calvino himself calls his list an "absurd hodgepodge," and notes: "I had fun imagining that among these terribly incongruous objects there ran a mysterious bond whose nature I would have to guess."[33] But without doubt the most deliberately chaotic of all incongruous lists is the list of animals in the Chinese encyclopedia entitled *The Celestial Emporium of Benevolent Knowledge*, invented by Borges and mentioned by Michel Foucault at the beginning of his preface to *The Order of Things*. The encyclopedia proposes that animals be divided into: (a) those that belong to the emperor; (b) those that have been embalmed; (c) those that are trained; (d) suckling pigs; (e) mermaids; (f) creatures of myth and fable; (g) stray dogs; (h) those that are included in this classification; (i) those that tremble as if they were mad; (j) those that are innumerable; (k) those drawn with a very fine camel's-hair brush; (l) etcetera; (m) those that have just broken the flower vase; (n) those that, from a distance, resemble flies.[34]

Having considered examples of coherent excess and chaotic enumeration, we realize that, compared to the lists of antiquity, these reveal something different. As we have seen, Homer fell back on the list because he lacked the words to do justice to his theme, and the topos of the ineffable dominated the poetics of lists for many centuries. But on looking at the lists drawn up by Joyce and Borges, we see that they made lists not because they didn't know what to say, but because they wanted to say things out of a love of excess, an urge toward hubris, and a greed for words, for the joyous (and rarely obsessive) science of the plural and the limitless. The list becomes a way of reshuffling the world, almost putting into practice Tesauro's method of accumulating properties in order to bring out new relationships between disparate things, and in any case to cast doubt on those accepted by common sense. In this way, the chaotic list becomes one of the modes of that breakdown of form set in motion in various ways by Futurism, Cubism, Dadaism, Surrealism, and the New Realism.

Borges's list, furthermore, not only challenges all criteria of congruity, but plays deliberately on the paradoxes of set theory. His list actually defies any reasonable criterion of congruity, because one cannot understand what sense there could be in putting that "etcetera" not at the end of the series, in place of additional elements, but *among* the items of the list itself. And this is not the only problem. The thing that makes the list really unsettling is that, among the items it classifies, it also includes "those included in the present classification." A student of mathematical logic immediately recognizes here the paradox formulated by the young Bertrand Russell as an objection to Frege: if a set is normal when it does not also include itself (the set of all cats is not a cat, but a concept) and if a set is non-normal when it is an element of itself (the set of all concepts is a concept), how can we define *the set of all normal sets?* If it were normal, we would have an incomplete set, because it does not also include itself; if it were non-normal, we would have an illogical set, because among all the normal sets, we would have also included a non-normal set. Borges's classification plays with this paradox. Either the classification of the animals is a normal set and hence must not contain itself—but self-inclusion does occur in Borges's list; or it is a non-normal set, and then the list would be incongruent because something would appear among the animals that is not an animal—it is a set.

I wonder if I ever designed a *truly* chaotic list. By way of an answer, I shall say that genuine chaotic lists can be written only by poets. Novelists are obliged to represent something that happens in a given space and time, and in so doing they always design a sort of framework within which any incongruous element is in some way "glued" to all the others. As an example, I would like to propose a sort of stream of consciousness by Yambo, the protagonist of *The Mysterious Flame of Queen Loana.* Yambo has lost his personal memory and has saved only the cultural memory, by which he is obsessed, though he cannot recall anything about himself or his family. At a certain moment, in a sort of delirium, he creates an utterly incoherent collage of miscellaneous poetic quotations. The list certainly sounds chaotic, because the sensation of mental chaos was precisely what I wanted to evoke. But if the thoughts of my character were chaotic, my list was even more so, because it was intended to represent a devastated mind:

I stroked the children and could smell their odor, without being able to define it except to say that it was tender. All that came to mind was *there are perfumes as fresh as a child's flesh.* And indeed my head was not empty, it was a maelstrom of memories that were not mine: the marchioness went out at five o'clock in the middle of the journey of our life, Abraham begat Isaac and Isaac begat Jacob and Jacob begat the man of La Mancha, and that was when I saw the pendulum, betwixt a smile and tear, on the branch of Lake Como where late the sweet birds sang, the snows of yesteryear softly falling into the dark mutinous Shannon waves, *messieurs les Anglais je me suis couché de bonne heure,* though words cannot heal the women come and go, here we shall make Italy or a kiss is just a kiss, *tu quoque alea,* a man without qualities fights and runs away, brothers of Italy ask not what you can do for your country, the plow that makes the furrow will live to fight another day, I mean a Nose by any other name, Italy is made now the rest is commentary, *mi espíritu se purifica en Paris con aguacero,* don't ask us for the word crazed with light, we'll have our battle in the shade and suddenly it's evening, around my heart three ladies' arms I sing, oh Valentino Valentino wherefore art thou, happy families are all alike said the bridegroom to the bride, Guido I wish that mother died today, I recognized the trembling of man's first disobedience, *de la musique où marchent des colombes,* go little book to where the lemons blossom, once upon a time there lived Achilles son of Peleus, and the earth was without form and too much with us, *Licht mehr licht über alles,* Contessa, what oh what is life? and Jill came tumbling after. Names, names, names: Angelo Dall'Oca Bianca, Lord Brummell, Pindar, Flaubert, Disraeli, Remigio, Zena, Jurassic, Fattori, Straparola and the pleasant nights, de Pompadour, Smith and Wesson, Rosa Luxemburg, Zeno Cosini, Palma the Elder, Archaeopteryx, Ciceruacchio, Matthew Mark Luke John, Pinocchio, Justine, Maria Goretti, Thaïs the whore with the shitty fingernails, Osteoporosis, Saint Honoré, Bactria Ecbatana Persepolis Susa Arbela, Alexander and the Gordian knot. The encyclopedia was tumbling down on me, its pages loose, and I felt like waving my hands the way one does amid a swarm of bees.[35]

Mass-Media Lists

The poetics of the list also pervade many aspects of mass culture, but with intentions different from those of avant-garde art. We need only think of those cinematic exemplars of the visual list—the parade of girls adorned with ostrich feathers coming down the staircase in the film *Ziegfeld Follies* (1945), the famous water ballet in *Bathing Beauty* (1944), the lines of dancing girls in *Footlight Parade* (1933), the models who file past in *Roberta* (1935)—and the modern fashion shows of the great designers.

Here, the succession of bewitching creatures is intended merely to suggest abundance, a need to satisfy the desire for the blockbuster, to show not only one glamorous image but a great many of them, to provide the user with an inexhaustible reserve of voluptuous appeal, just as potentates of old adorned themselves with cascades of jewels. The technique of the list is not intended to call the social order into question; on the contrary, its purpose is to reiterate that the universe of abundance and consumption, available to all, represents the only possible model of ordered society.

Providing lists of different beauties has something to do with the characteristics of the society that generated the mass media. It reminds us of Karl Marx, who at the beginning of *Das Kapital* says: "The wealth of those societies in which the Capitalist mode of production prevails presents itself as an immense accumulation of commodities." Think of the shop-window which displays an extravagant wealth of objects and suggests that inside there are many more; or a trade fair, with goods from all over the world; or the Parisian arcades *(passages)* celebrated by Walter Benjamin—corridors with glass roofs and inlaid-marble walls, containing rows of elegant shops —which the old nineteenth-century Parisian guidebooks described as a world in miniature; and finally the department store (extolled by Zola in his novel *Au Bonheur des dames*), a true list in itself.

In *The Mysterious Flame of Queen Loana,* which deals mainly with a quasi-archaeological retrieval of memorabilia from the 1930s, I frequently resorted to the catalogue (once again made chaotic by frantic collage). Let me quote a passage where I evoke the mass of kitschy songs with which the national radio broadcasts strafed my youthful ears:

> Just as if the radio were singing to me all by itself, without my having to turn any knobs. I started the first record and stood swaying by the window, with the starry sky above me, to the sounds of so much good bad music that something should have woken up inside me.

Tonight the stars are shining by the thousand. . . . One night, with the stars and you . . . Speak, oh speak in the starlight so clear, whisper sweet words in my ear, under the spell of love . . . Beneath the Antilles night, with the stars burning bright, there flowed the streaming light of love . . . Mailù, under the Singapore sky, its golden stars dreamily high, we fell in love, you and I . . . Beneath the maze of stars that gazes down on all of this, beneath the craze of stars I want to give your lips a kiss. . . . With you, without, we sing to the stars and the moon, you can't rule it out, good fortune may come to me soon. . . . Harbor moon, love is sweet if you never learn, Venice the moon and you, you and me all alone in the night, you and me humming a tune, . . . Hungarian sky, melancholy sigh, I'm thinking of you with infinite love. . . . I wander where the sky is always blue, listening to thrushes as they flutter in the bushes, their twittering coming through.[36]

Books, Books, Books . . .

A library catalogue, as I said above, is an example of a practical list because the books of a library are finite in number. An exception, of course, would be the catalogue of an infinite library.

How many books are in the Library of Babel so fancifully described by Borges? One of the properties of Borges's library is that it displays books containing all the possible combinations of twenty-five orthographic symbols, so that we cannot imagine any combination of characters that the library has not foreseen. In 1622 Paul Guldin, in *Problema arithmeticum de rerum combinationibus,* calculated how many words could have been produced with the twenty-three letters of the alphabet in use at the time. He combined them two by two, three by three, and so on, until he got to words twenty-three letters long, without taking into account repetitions and without worrying about whether the words that could be generated made sense or were even pronounceable; and he arrived at a number in excess of seventy thousand billion billions (to write them would have taken more than a million billion billion letters). If we were to write all these words in volumes of one thousand pages each, at one hundred lines per page and sixty characters per line, we would need 257 million billion volumes of this kind. And if we wished to put them in a library equipped with cubic storage spaces measuring 432 feet on a side, each capable of housing 32 million volumes, then we would need 8,052,122,350 such libraries. But what realm could contain all these buildings? If we calculate the surface available on the entire planet, we find that the Earth could accommodate only 7,575,213,799 of them!

Many others, from Marin Mersenne to Gottfried Leibniz, have performed calculations of this kind. The dream of an infinite library encourages writers to try compiling examples of an infinite list of titles—and the most convincing specimen of such an infinity is a list of invented, nonexistent titles, meaning that it is possible to conceive of an infinite invention. This is the kind of thrilling venture that can give us, say, the list of the (fake) books in the Library of St. Victor, such as Rabelais presents them in *Pantagruel: The For Godsake of Salvation; The Codpiece of the Law; The Slipshoe of the Decretals; The Pomegranate of Vice; The Clew-Bottom of Theology; The Duster or Foxtail-Flap of Preachers, Composed by Turlupin; The Churning Ballock of the Valiant; The Henbane of the Bishops; Marmotretus de baboonis et apis, cum commento Dorbellis; Decretum Universitatis Parisiensis super gorgiasitate muliercularum ad placitum; The Apparition of Sancte Geltrude to a Nun of Poissy, Being in Travail at the Bringing Forth of a Child; Ars honeste fartandi in societate per Marcum Corvinum; Quaestio subtilissima, utrum Chimaera in vacuo bonbinans possit comedere secundas intentiones;* and so on, for approximately one hundred fifty titles.[37]

But we can feel the same vertigo of infinity when we encounter lists of titles of real books, as when Diogenes Laertius itemizes all the books written by

Theophrastus. The reader has difficulty conceiving of such a vast collection—not just the content of the books, but even their mere titles:

> Three books of the First Analytics; seven of the Second Analytics; one book of the Analysis of Syllogisms; one book, an Epitome of Analytics; two books, Topics for referring things to First Principles; one book, an Examination of Speculative Questions about Discussions; one on Sensations; one addressed to Anaxagoras; one on the Doctrines of Anaxagoras; one on the Doctrines of Anaximenes; one on the Doctrines of Archelaus; one on Salt, Nitre, and Alum; two on Petrifactions; one on Indivisible Lines; two on Hearing; one on Words; one on the Differences between Virtues; one on Kingly Power; one on the Education of a King; three on Lives; one on Old Age; one on the Astronomical System of Democritus; one on Meteorology; one on Images or Phantoms; one on Juices, Complexions, and Flesh; one on the Description of the World; one on Men; one, a Collection of the Sayings of Diogenes; three books of Definitions; one treatise on Love; another treatise on Love; one book on Happiness; two books on Species; on Epilepsy, one; on Enthusiasm, one; on Empedocles, one; eighteen books of Epicheiremes; three books of Objections; one book on the Voluntary; two books, being an Abridgment of Plato's Polity; one on the Difference of the Voices of Similar Animals; one on Sudden Appearances; one on Animals which Bite or Sting; one on such Animals as are said to

be Jealous; one on those which live on Dry Land; one on those which Change their Colour; one on those which live in Holes; seven on Animals in General; one on Pleasure according to the Definition of Aristotle; seventy-four books of Propositions; one treatise on Hot and Cold; one essay on Giddiness and Vertigo and Sudden Dimness of Sight; one on Perspiration; one on Affirmation and Denial; the Callisthenes, or an essay on Mourning, one; on Labours, one; on Motion, three; on Stones, one; on Pestilences, one; on Fainting Fits, one; the Megaric Philosopher, one; on Melancholy, one; on Mines, two; on Honey, one; a collection of the Doctrines of Metrodorus, one; two books on those Philosophers who have treated of Meteorology; on Drunkenness, one; twenty-four books of Laws, in alphabetical order; ten books, being an Abridgment of Laws; one on Definitions; one on Smells; one on Wine and Oil; eighteen books of Primary Propositions; three books on Lawgivers; six books of Political Disquisitions; a treatise on Politicals, with reference to occasions as they arise, four books; four books of Political Customs; on the best Constitution, one; five books of a Collection of Problems; on Proverbs, one; on Concretion and Liquefaction, one; on Fire, two; on Spirits, one; on Paralysis, one; on Suffocation, one; on Aberration of Intellect, one; on the Passions, one; on Signs, one; two books of Sophisms; one on the Solution of Syllogisms; two books of Topics; two on Punishment; one on Hair; one on Tyranny; three on Water; one on Sleep and Dreams; three on Friendship; two on Liberality; three on Nature; eighteen on Questions of Natural Philosophy; two books, being an Abridgment of Natural Philosophy; eight more books on Natural Philosophy; one treatise addressed to Natural Philosophers; two books on the History of Plants; eight books on the Causes of Plants; five on Juices; one on Mistaken Pleasures; one, Investigation of a proposition concerning the Soul; one on Unskillfully Adduced Proofs; one on Simple Doubts; one on Harmonies; one on Virtue; one entitled Occasions or Contradictions; one on Denial; one on Opinion; one on the Ridiculous; two called Soirées; two books of Divisions; one on Differences; one on Acts of Injustice; one on Calumny; one on Praise; one on Skill; three books of Epistles; one on Self-produced Animals; one on Selection; one entitled the Praises of the Gods; one on Festivals; one on Good Fortune; one on Enthymemes; one on Inventions; one on Moral Schools; one book of Moral Characters; one treatise on Tumult; one on History: one on the Judgment Concerning Syllogisms; one on Flattery; one on the Sea; one essay, addressed to Cassander, Concerning Kingly Power; one on Comedy; one on Meteors; one on Style; one book called a Collection of Sayings; one book of Solutions; three books on Music; one on Metres; the Megades, one; on Laws, one; on Violations of Law, one; a collection of the Sayings and Doctrines of Xenocrates, one; one book of Conversations; on an Oath, one; one of Oratorical Precepts; one on Riches; one on Poetry; one being a collection of Political, Ethical, Physical, and Amatory Problems; one book of Proverbs; one book, being a Collection of General Problems; one on Problems in Natural Philosophy; one on Example; one on Proposition and Exposition; a second treatise on Poetry; one on the Wise Men; one on Counsel; one on Solecisms; one on Rhetorical Art; a collection of sixty-one figures of Oratorical Art; one book on Hypocrisy; six books of a Commentary on Aristotle; sixteen books of Opinions on Natural Philosophy; one book, being an Abridgment of Opinions on Natural Philosophy; one on Gratitude; one called Moral Characters; one on Truth and Falsehood; six on the History of Divine Things; three on the Gods; four on the History of Geometry; six books, being an Abridgment of the work of Aristotle on Animals; two books of Epicheiremes; three books of Propositions; two on Kingly Power; one on Causes; one on Democritus; one on Calumny; one on Generation; one on the Intellect and Moral Character of Animals; two on Motion; four on Sight; two on Definitions; one on being given in Marriage; one on the Greater and the Less; one on Music; one on Divine Happiness; one addressed to the Philosophers of the Academy; one Exhortatory Treatise; one discussing how a City may be best Governed; one called Commentaries; one on the Crater of Mount Etna in Sicily; one on Admitted Facts; one on Problems in Natural History; one, What Are the Different Manners of Acquiring Knowledge; three on Telling Lies; one book, which is a preface to the Topics; one addressed to Aeschylus; six books of a History of Astronomy; one book of the History of Arithmetic relating to Increasing Numbers; one called the Acicharus; one on Judicial Discourses; one on Calumny; one volume of Letters to Astyceron, Phanias, and Nicanor; one book on Piety; one called the Evias; one on Circumstances; one volume entitled Familiar Conversations; one on the Education of Children; another on the same subject, discussed in a different manner; one on Education, called also A Treatise on Virtue, or on Temperance; one book of Exhortations; one on Numbers; one consisting of Definitions referring to the Enunciation of Syllogisms: one on Heaven; two on Politics; two on Nature, on Fruits, and on Animals. And these works contain, in all, two hundred and thirty-two thousand nine hundred and eight lines. These, then, are the books which Theophrastus composed.[38]

I was probably thinking of such lists when I included in *The Name of the Rose* an uninterrupted list of books held in the library of the abbey. And the fact that I mentioned real books (circulating at that time in monastic collections), rather than invented titles like the ones Rabelais cites, does not alter the impression of prayer, mantra, and litany that a list of books can suggest. The taste for book lists has fascinated many writers, from Cervantes to Huysmans and Calvino. Bibliophiles read the catalogues of antiquarian bookshops (which are certainly meant to be practical lists) as fascinating portrayals of a Land of Cockaigne, a realm of desire, and they get as much pleasure out of this as a reader of Jules Verne gets from exploring the silent depths of the oceans and encountering fabulous sea monsters.

Today, we can actually encounter an infinite list of titles: the World Wide Web really is the Mother of All Lists, infinite by definition because it is in constant evolution, both web and labyrinth. Of all vertigos, the one it promises us is the most mystical; it is almost totally virtual, and really offers us a catalogue of information that makes us feel wealthy and omnipotent. The only snag is that we don't know which of its elements refer to data from the real world and which do not. There is no longer any distinction between truth and error.

Is it still possible to invent new lists if, when I ask Google to do a search with the keyword "list," I find a list of nearly 2.2 billion sites?

But if a list is to suggest infinity, it cannot be outrageously long. I feel dizzy enough when I review the titles of only some of the books I mention in *The Name of the Rose*: *De pentagono Salomonis; Ars loquendi et intelligendi in lingua hebraica; De rebus metallicis,* by Roger of Hereford; *Algebra,* by Al-Kuwarizmi; *Punica,* by Silius Italicus; *Gesta francorum; De laudibus sanctae crucis,* by Rabanus Maurus; *Giordani de aetate mundi et hominis reservatis singulis litteris per singulos libros ab A usque ad Z; Quinti Sereni de medicamentis; Phaenomena; Liber Aesopi de natura animalium; Liber Aethici peronymi de cosmographia; Libri tres quos Arculphus episcopus Adamnano escipiente de locis sanctis ultramarinis designavit conscribendos; Libellus Q. Iulii Hilarionis de origine mundi; Solini Polyhistor de situ orbis terrarum et mirabilibus; Almagesthus . . .*

Or the list of novels about Fantômas: *Fantômas; Juve contre Fantômas; Le Mort qui tue; L'Agent secret; Un Roi prisonnier de Fantômas; Le Policier apache; Le Pendu de Londres; La Fille de Fantômas; Le Fiacre de nuit; La Main coupée; L'Arrestation de Fantômas; Le Magistrat cambrioleur; La Vivrée du crime; La Mort de Juve; L'Evadée de Saint-Lazare; La Disparition de Fandor; Les Souliers du mort; Le Mariage de Fantômas; L'Assassin de Lady Beltham; La Guêpe rouge; Le Train perdu; Les Amours d'un prince; Le Bouquet tragique; Le Jockey masqué; Le Voleur d'or; Le Cadavre géant; Le Faiseur de reines; Le Cercueil vide; Le Série rouge; L'Hôtel du crime; La Cravate de chanvre; La Fin de Fantômas.*

Or the (partial) catalogue of the stories of Sherlock Holmes: "A Case of Identity," "A Scandal in Bohemia," "The Red-Headed League," "The Three Students," "The Boscombe Valley Mystery," "The Five Orange Pips," "The Man with the Twisted Lip," "The Adventure of the Blue Carbuncle," "The Adventure of the Speckled Band," "The Adventure of the Engineer's Thumb," "The Adventure of the Noble Bachelor," "The Adventure of the Copper Beeches," "Silver Blaze," "The Adventure of the Blanched Soldier," "The Adventure of the Creeping Man," "The Adventure of the Illustrious Client," "The Adventure of the Lion's Mane," "The Adventure of the Mazarin Stone," "The Adventure of the Retired Colourman," "The Adventure of the Sussex Vampire," "The Adventure of the Three Gables," "The Adventure of the Three Garridebs," "The Adventure of the Veiled Lodger," "The Adventure of the Beryl Coronet," "The Cardboard Box," "The Dying Detective," "The Empty House," "The Final Problem," "The Adventure of the *Gloria Scott*," "The Greek Interpreter," "The Hound of the Baskervilles," "The Musgrave Ritual," "A Study in Scarlet," "The Adventure of the Naval Treaty," "The Norwood Builder," "The Problem of Thor Bridge," "The Red Circle," "The Reigate Squires," "The Resident Patient," "The Second Stain," "The Sign of the Four," "The Six Napoleons," "The Solitary Cyclist," "The Stock-Broker's Clerk," "The Valley of Fear," . . . *Amen*.

Lists: a pleasure to read and to write. These are the confessions of a young writer.

Notes

Index

Notes

1. WRITING FROM LEFT TO RIGHT

1. Some give up versifying only a little past the age of eighteen, like Rimbaud.

2. In the late 1950s and early 1960s, I wrote several parodies and other prose works — now collected in the volume *Misreadings* (New York: Harcourt, 1993). But I considered them mere *divertissements*.

3. See Umberto Eco, "Come scrivo," in Maria Teresa Serafini, ed., *Come si scrive un romanzo* (Milan: Bompiani, 1996).

4. Linda Hutcheon, "Eco's Echoes: Ironizing the (Post) Modern," in Norma Bouchard and Veronica Pravadelli, eds., *Umberto Eco's Alternative* (New York: Peter Lang, 1998); Linda Hutcheon, *A Poetics of Postmodernism* (London: Routledge, 1988); Brian McHale, *Constructing Postmodernism* (London: Routledge, 1992); Remo Ceserani, "Eco's (Post)modernist Fictions," in Bouchard and Pravadelli, *Umberto Eco's Alternative*.

5. Charles A. Jencks, *The Language of Post-Modern Architecture* (Wisbech, U.K.: Balding and Mansell, 1978), 6.

6. Charles A. Jencks, *What Is Post-Modernism?* (London: Art and Design, 1986), 14–15. See also Charles A. Jencks, ed., *The Post-Modern Reader* (New York: St. Martin's, 1992).

2. AUTHOR, TEXT, AND INTERPRETERS

A version of Chapter 2 was delivered as a lecture entitled "The Author and His Interpreters" at the Italian Academy for Advanced Studies in America, Columbia University, 1996.

1. Umberto Eco, *The Open Work* (Cambridge, Mass.: Harvard University Press, 1989).

2. See Jacques Derrida, "Signature Event Context" (1971), *Glyph*, 1 (1977): 172–197, reprinted in Derrida, *Limited Inc.*, trans. Samuel Weber and Jeffrey Mehlman (Evanston, Ill.: Northwestern University Press, 1988); and John Searle, "Reiterating the Differences: A Reply to Derrida," *Glyph*, 1 (1977): 198–208, reprinted in Searle, *The Construction of Social Reality* (New York: Free Press, 1995).

3. See Philip L. Graham, "Late Historical Events," *A Wake Newslitter* (October 1964): 13–14; Nathan Halper, "Notes on Late Historical Events," *A Wake Newslitter* (October 1965): 15–16.

4. Ruth von Phul, "Late Historical Events," *A Wake Newslitter* (December 1965): 14–15.

5. It must be remarked, however, that in terms of syllabic quantity, the *o* of "Roma" is long, so that the initial dactyl of the hexameter would not work properly. "Rosa" is therefore the correct reading.

6. Helena Costiucovich, "Umberto Eco: Imja Rosi," *Sovriemiennaja hudoziestviennaja litieratura za rubiezom*, 5 (1982): 101ff.

7. Robert F. Fleissner, *A Rose by Another Name: A Survey of Literary Flora from Shakespeare to Eco* (West Cornwall, U.K.: Locust Hill Press, 1989), 139.

8. Giosue Musca, "La camicia del nesso," *Quaderni Medievali*, 27 (1989).

9. A. R. Luria, *The Man with a Shattered World: The History*

of a Brain Wound (Cambridge, Mass.: Harvard University Press, 1987).

3. SOME REMARKS ON FICTIONAL CHARACTERS

1. Umberto Eco, *Foucault's Pendulum,* trans. William Weaver (New York: Harcourt, 1989), ch. 57.

2. By the way, a real Faria existed, and Dumas was inspired by this curious Portuguese priest. But the real Faria was interested in mesmerism and had very little to do with the mentor of Monte Cristo. Dumas used to take some of his characters from history (as he did with d'Artagnan), but his readers were not expected to be concerned with the real-life attributes of those characters.

3. Years ago I visited the fortress and saw not only what was called Monte Cristo's cell, but also the tunnel allegedly dug by the abbé Faria.

4. Alexandre Dumas, *Viva Garibaldi! Une odyssée en 1860* (Paris: Fayard, 2002), ch. 4.

5. A gentle and sensitive friend of mine used to say: "Every time I see a waving flag in a movie, I cry—regardless of the nationality." In any case, the fact that human beings are moved by fictional characters has given rise to a vast literature, in both psychology and narratology. For a comprehensive overview, see Margit Sutrop, "Sympathy, Imagination, and the Reader's Emotional Response to Fiction," in Jürgen Schlaeger and Gesa Stedman, eds., *Representations of Emotions* (Tübingen: Günter Narr Verlag, 1999), 29–42. See also Margit Sutrop, *Fiction and Imagination* (Paderborn: Mentis Verlag, 2000), 5.2; Colin Radford, "How Can We Be Moved by the Fate of Anna Karenina?" *Proceedings of the Aristotelian Society,* 69, suppl.

(1975): 77; Francis Farrugia, "Syndrome narratif et arché-
types romanesques de la sentimentalité: Don Quichotte,
Madame Bovary, un discours du pape, et autres histoires,"
in Farrugia et al., *Emotions et sentiments: Une construction
sociale* (Paris: L'Harmattan, 2008).

6. See Gregory Currie, *Image and Mind* (Cambridge: Cambridge University Press, 1995). Catharsis, as defined by
Aristotle, is a sort of emotional illusion: it depends on
our identification with the heroes of tragic drama, so that
we feel pity and terror when witnessing what happens to
them.

7. For a careful and complete discussion of the ontological
point of view, see Carola Barbero, *Madame Bovary: Something Like a Melody* (Milan: Albo Versorio, 2005). Barbero
does a good job of clarifying the difference between an
ontological and a cognitive approach: "Object Theory
has no interest in knowing how we cognitively grasp objects that do not exist. In fact, it focuses only on objects in
their absolute generality and independently from their
possible way of givenness" (65).

8. See John Searle, "The Logical Status of Fictional Discourse," *New Literary History*, 6, no. 2 (Winter 1975):
319–332.

9. Jaakko Hintikka, "Exploring Possible Worlds," in Sture
Allén, ed., *Possible Worlds in Humanities, Arts and Sciences,*
vol. 65 of *Proceedings of the Nobel Symposium* (New York:
De Gruyter, 1989), 55.

10. Lubomir Dolezel, "Possible Worlds and Literary Fiction," in Allén, *Possible Worlds,* 233.

11. For instance, President George W. Bush said at a press
conference on September 24, 2001, that "border relations

between Canada and Mexico have never been better." See usinfo.org/wf-archive/2001/010924/epf109.htm.

12. Cited in Samuel Delany, "Generic Protocols," in Teresa de Lauretis, ed., *The Technological Imagination* (Madison, Wis.: Coda Press, 1980).

13. On a narrative possible world as being "small" and "parasitic," see Umberto Eco, *The Limits of Interpretation* (Bloomington: Indiana University Press, 1990), chapter entitled "Small Worlds."

14. As I said in *Six Walks in the Fictional Woods* (Cambridge, Mass.: Harvard University Press, 1994), ch. 5, readers are more or less eager to accept certain violations of conditions in the real world, according to the state of their encyclopedic information. Alexandre Dumas, in *The Three Musketeers,* which is set in the 1600s, had his character Aramis living on the Rue Servandoni—an impossibility, since the architect Giovanni Servandoni, for whom the street was named, lived and worked a century later. But readers could accept that information without being disconcerted, because very few of them knew anything about Servandoni. If, in contrast, Dumas had said that Aramis lived on the Rue Bonaparte, readers would have had a right to feel uneasy.

15. See, for instance, Roman Ingarden, *Das literarische Kunstwerk* (Halle: Niemayer Verlag, 1931); in English, *The Literary Work of Art,* trans. George G. Grabowicz (Evanston, Ill.: Northwestern University Press, 1973).

16. Stendhal, *The Red and the Black,* trans. Horace B. Samuel (London: Kegan Paul, 1916), 464.

17. On these two bullets, see Jacques Geninasca, *La Parole littéraire* (Paris: PUF, 1997), II, 3.

18. See, for instance, Umberto Eco, *Kant and the Platypus*, trans. Alastair McEwen (New York: Harcourt, 1999), in particular sect. 1.9.

19. But if Anna is an artifact, her nature is different from that of other artifacts such as chairs or ships. See Amie L. Thomasson, "Fictional Characters and Literary Practices," *British Journal of Aesthetics*, 43, no. 2 (April 2002): 138–157. Fictional artifacts are not physical entities and lack a spatio-temporal location.

20. See, for instance, Umberto Eco, *Semiotics and the Philosophy of Language* (Bloomington: Indiana University Press, 1984), 2.3.3; and idem, *The Limits of Interpretation* (Bloomington: Indiana University Press, 1990).

21. Philippe Doumenc, *Contre-enquête sur la mort d'Emma Bovary* (Paris: Actes Sud, 2007).

22. See Eco, *Six Walks in the Fictional Woods*, 126.

23. See, for instance, Aislinn Simpson, "Winston Churchill Didn't Really Exist," *Telegraph*, February 4, 2008.

24. For a history of the idea of social objects, from Giambattista Vico and Thomas Reid to John Searle, see Maurizio Ferraris, "Scienze sociali," in Ferraris, ed., *Storia dell'ontologia* (Milan: Bompiani, 2008), 475–490.

25. See, for instance, John Searle, "Proper Names," *Mind*, 67 (1958): 172.

26. See Roman Ingarden, *Time and Modes of Being*, trans. Helen R. Michejda (Springfield, Ill.: Charles C. Thomas, 1964); and idem, *The Literary Work of Art*. For a criticism of Ingarden's position, see Amie L. Thomasson, "Ingarden and the Ontology of Cultural Objects," in Arkadiusz Chrudzimski, ed., *Existence, Culture, and Persons: The Ontology of Roman Ingarden* (Frankfurt: Ontos Verlag, 2005).

27. Barbero, *Madame Bovary,* 45–61.

28. Woody Allen, "The Kugelmass Episode," in Allen, *Side Effects* (New York: Random House, 1980).

29. On these problems, see Patrizia Violi, *Meaning and Experience,* trans. Jeremy Carden (Bloomington: Indiana University Press, 2001), IIB and III. See also Eco, *Kant and the Platypus,* 199, 3.7.

30. Peter Strawson, "On Referring," *Mind,* 59 (1950).

31. Obviously, encyclopedias must be kept up to date. On May 4, 1821, the public encyclopedia had to record Napoleon as a former emperor still living in exile on the island of Saint Helena.

32. In cases that are difficult to check *de visu* (for instance, if *p* is asserting that Obama visited Baghdad yesterday), we rely on "prostheses" (such as newspapers or TV programs) that allegedly should enable us to check what really happened *in this world,* even though the event was beyond our perceptual reach.

33. One might be tempted to claim that mathematical entities are likewise immune to revision. Yet even the concept of parallel lines changed after the advent of non-Euclidean geometries, and our ideas about Fermat's Theorem changed after 1994 thanks to the work of the British mathematician Andrew Wiles.

34. To be rigorous, we should say that the expression "Jesus Christ" refers to two different objects, and that when somebody utters this name, we should—in order to give meaning to the utterance—determine what kind of religious (or nonreligious) beliefs the speaker adheres to.

35. On these questions, see Umberto Eco, *The Role of the Reader* (Bloomington: Indiana University Press, 1979).

4. MY LISTS

1. See Umberto Eco, *The Infinity of Lists,* trans. Alastair McEwen (New York: Rizzoli International, 2009).

2. On the difference between "pragmatic" and "literary" lists, see Robert E. Belknap, *The List* (New Haven: Yale University Press, 2004). A valuable anthology of literary lists can also be found in Francis Spufford, ed., *The Chatto Book of Cabbages and Kings: Lists in Literature* (London: Chatto and Windus, 1989). Belknap thinks that "pragmatic" lists can be extended to infinity (a telephone directory, say, can become larger every year, and we can make a shopping list longer on our way to the store), whereas the lists he calls "literary" are in fact closed owing to the formal constraints of the work that contains them (meter, rhyme, sonnet form, and so on). It seems to me that this argument can easily be turned on its head. Insofar as practical lists designate a finite series of things *at a given moment,* they are necessarily finite. They can certainly be increased, as happens with a telephone directory, but the phone book of 2008, compared to the one of 2007, is simply *another* list. In contrast, despite the constraints involved in artistic techniques, all the poetic lists I shall quote below could be expanded *ad infinitum.*

3. Ennodius, *Carmina,* Book 9, sect. 323c, in *Patrologia Latina,* ed. J.-P. Migne, vol. 63 (Paris, 1847).

4. Cicero, "First Oration against Lucius Catilina," in *The Orations of Marcus Tullius Cicero,* trans. C. D. Yonge, vol. 2 (London: G. Bell and Sons, 1917), 279–280 (sect. 1).

5. Ibid., 282 (sect. 3).

6. From Wislawa Szymborska, *Nothing Twice,* trans. Stanis-

law Baranczak and Clare Cavanagh (Krakow: Wydaw-
nictwo Literackie, 1997).

7. Unfortunately, the asyndeton gets lost in the first English
   translation, by William Stewart Rose (eighteenth century), which reads: "Of loves and ladies, knights and arms,
   I sing,/ of courtesies, and many a daring feat."

8. Italo Calvino, *The Nonexistent Knight,* trans. Archibald
   Colquhoun (New York: Harcourt, 1962).

9. François Rabelais, *Gargantua,* trans. Sir Thomas Urquhart of Cromarty (1653) and Peter Antony Motteux
   (1693–1708) (Chicago: Encyclopaedia Britannica, 1990),
   ch. 22, "The Games of Gargantua."

10. James Joyce, *Ulysses,* ed. Hans Walter Gabler (New York:
    Vintage, 1986), 592–593 (Book 3, ch. 2).

11. Umberto Eco, *Misreadings,* trans. William Weaver (New
    York: Harcourt, 1993).

12. Umberto Eco, *The Name of the Rose,* trans. William
    Weaver (New York: Harcourt, 1983), ch. 3.

13. I may have been wrong about this. Though the dates are
    uncertain, it is possible that the first list is the entire
    Theogony, by Hesiod.

14. See Giuseppe Ledda, "Elenchi impossibili: Cataloghi e
    topos dell'indicibilità," unpublished; and idem, *La Guerra
    della lingua: Ineffabilità, retorica e narrativa nella Comme-
    dia di Dante* (Ravenna: Longo, 2002).

15. Dante, *Paradise,* trans. Henry Francis Cary (London:
    Barfield, 1814), Canto 28, lines 91–92.

16. Umberto Eco, *The Island of the Day Before,* trans. Wil-
    liam Weaver (New York: Harcourt, 1995), pp. 407–410
    (ch. 32). The experienced reader will see in the closing
    sentence a case not only of hypotyposis but also of ek-

phrasis: it describes a typical head painted by Arcimboldo.

17. Walt Whitman, *Leaves of Grass,* Part 12, "Song of the Broad-Axe." See in particular the chapter devoted to Whitman in Robert E. Belknap, *The List* (New Haven: Yale University Press, 2004).

18. James Joyce, "Anna Livia Plurabelle," trans. James Joyce and Nino Frank (1938), reprinted in Joyce, *Scritti italiani* (Milan: Mondadori, 1979).

19. James Joyce, "Anna Livie Plurabelle," trans. Samuel Beckett, Alfred Perron, Philippe Soupault, Paul Léon, Eugène Jolas, Ivan Goll, and Adrienne Monnier, with the collaboration of Joyce, *Nouvelle Revue Française,* May 1, 1931.

20. My collage is based on the translation by Andrew Hurley, in *Collected Fictions of Jorge Luis Borges* (New York: Viking, 1998).

21. Umberto Eco, *Baudolino,* trans. William Weaver (New York: Harcourt Brace, 2001), 31.

22. Umberto Eco, *Foucault's Pendulum,* trans. William Weaver (New York: Harcourt Brace, 1998), pp. 7–8 (ch. 1); pp. 575–579 (ch. 112).

23. We shall not tackle here the age-old problem of *specific difference,* by virtue of which humans can be distinguished as rational animals in contrast to the other, irrational animals. On this, see Umberto Eco, *Semiotics and the Philosophy of Language* (Bloomington: Indiana University Press, 1984), ch. 2. On the platypus, see idem, *Kant and the Platypus* (New York: Harcourt, 1999).

24. Naturally, a list by properties can also be intended in an evaluative sense. An example might be the eulogy for Tyre in Ezekiel 27, or the paean to England ("this sceptered isle . . .") in Act 2 of Shakespeare's *Richard II.* An-

other evaluative list by properties is the topos of the *laudatio puellae*—the representation of beautiful women—of which the noblest example is the Song of Songs. But we also come across it in modern authors such as Rubén Darío, in his "Canto a la Argentina," which is a veritable explosion of encomiastic lists in the style of Whitman. Similarly, there is the *vituperatio puellae* (or *vituperatio dominae*)—the description of ugly women—as in Horace or in Clément Marot. There are also descriptions of ugly men, as in Cyrano's famous tirade on his own nose, in Edmond Rostand's *Cyrano de Bergerac*.

25. See Umberto Eco, *The Search for a Perfect Language* (Oxford: Blackwell, 1995).

26. I follow the translation by Alastair McEwen in Eco, *The Infinity of Lists*.

27. See Leo Spitzer, *La Enumeración caotica en la poesia moderna* (Buenos Aires: Faculdad de Filosofía y Letras, 1945).

28. Eco, *Baudolino*, ch. 28, trans. William Weaver.

29. Louis-Ferdinand Céline, *Bagatelles pour un massacre*, trans. Alastair McEwan. Any translation of that rabidly anti-Semitic work has been forbidden by Céline's estate. A version is offered at vho.org/aaargh/fran/livres6/CELINEtrif.pdf (accessed August 20, 2010). Alastair McEwan, the translator of my book *The Infinity of Lists*, preferred to try a brand-new rendering. It's probably worth quoting the original (which smacks curiously of Captain Haddock's furious outbursts in *Tintin*): "Dine! Paradine! Crèvent! Boursouflent! Ventre dieu! . . . 487 millions! D'empalafiés cosacologues! Quid? Quid? Quod? Dans tous les chancres de Slavie! Quid? De Baltique slavigote en Blanche Altramer noire? Quam? Balkans! Visqueux! Ratagan! De concombres! . . . Mornes! Roteux!

De ratamerde! Je m'en pourfentre! . . . Je m'en pourfoutre! Gigantement! Je m'envole! Coloquinte! . . . Barbatoliers? Immensément! Volgaronoff! . . . Mongomoleux Tartaronesques! . . . Stakhanoviciants! . . . Culodovitch! . . . Quatre cent mille verstes myriamètres! . . . De steppes de condachiures, de peaux de Zébis-Laridon! . . . Ventre Poultre! Je m'en gratte tous les Vésuves! . . . Déluges! . . . Fongueux de margachiante! . . . Pour vos tout sales pots fiottés d'entzarinavés! . . . Stabiline! Vorokchiots! Surplus Déconfits! . . . Transbérie!"

30. See Detlev W. Schumann, "Enumerative Style and Its Significance in Whitman, Rilke, Werfel," *Modern Language Quarterly,* 3, no. 2 (June 1942): 171–204.

31. Spitzer, *La Enumeración caotica en la poesia moderna.*

32. Arthur Rimbaud, "Childhood," Part 3, trans. Louise Varèse (1946), *Illuminations,* www.mag4.net/Rimbaud/poesies/Childhood.html (accessed September 2, 2010).

33. Italo Calvino, "Il cielo di pietra," in *Tutte le cosmicomiche* (Milan: Mondadori, 1997), 314; in English, *The Complete Cosmicomics,* trans. Martin McLaughlin, Tim Parks, and William Weaver (New York: Penguin, 2009).

34. Jorge Luis Borges, "John Wilkins' Analytical Language," in Borges, *Selected Nonfictions,* ed. Eliot Weinberger, trans. Esther Allen et al. (New York: Viking Penguin, 1999). Michel Foucault, *Les Mots et les choses* (Paris: Gallimard, 1966); in English, *The Order of Things* (New York: Pantheon, 1970), preface.

35. Umberto Eco, *The Mysterious Flame of Queen Loana,* trans. Geoffrey Brock (New York: Harcourt, 2005), ch. 1. I feel a bit awkward citing this text as if it were mine. In the original Italian text, I cobbled together literary quotations easily recognizable by the average Italian reader,

and the translator had to "recreate" the compilation by choosing quotations that would be recognized by English readers. This is one of those cases in which the translator must avoid a literal translation so as to produce, in another language, the *same effect*. At any rate, Brock's text, though different from the original, gives a sense of my chaotic collage.

36. Ibid., ch. 8.

37. François Rabelais, *Pantagruel*, trans. Sir Thomas Urquhart of Cromarty and Peter Antony Motteux (Derby, U.K.: Moray Press, 1894), Book 1, ch. 7.

38. Diogenes Laertius, *The Lives and Opinions of Eminent Philosophers*, trans. C. D. Yonge (London: Bohn, 1853), Book 5, "Life of Theophrastus," 42–50.

Index